'If all mankind minus one were of one opinion, and only one person were of the contrary opinion, mankind would be no more justified in silencing that one person, than he, if he had the power, would be justified in silencing mankind.'

John Stuart Mill, *On Liberty*

'*Why Read Mill Today?* is a philosophical gem. John Skorupski answers the question of his title briefly, clearly, and persuasively. More remarkably still, he answers it in a way that illuminates Mill for the reader who has never read him, and yet should interest scholars who know Mill well.'

Peter Singer, Princeton University

'John Skorupski brilliantly describes Mill's place in the great sweep of ideas from the nineteenth century until the present day, leaving the reader in no doubt as to Mill's continuing huge significance. This is an engaging, accessible, and exciting book, which anyone seriously interested in ethics, politics, and the history of ideas should read.'

Roger Crisp, St Anne's College, Oxford

'John Skorupski is one of the leading scholars of Mill and nineteenth century philosophy. *Why Read Mill Today?* is a marvellously concise, accessible, and engaging discussion of the moral and political philosophy of John Stuart Mill, one which both situates Mill's views in their historical context and probes their continuing significance.'

lifornia, San Diego

Why Read Mill Today?

———— • ◆ • ————

John Stuart Mill is one of the greatest thinkers of the nineteenth century. But does he have anything to teach us today? His deep concern for freedom of the individual is thought by some to be outdated and inadequate to the cultural and religious complexities of life in the twenty-first century.

In this succinct and shrewd book, John Skorupski argues that Mill is a profound and inspiring social and political thinker from whom we still have much to learn. He reflects on Mill's central arguments in his most famous works, including *Utilitarianism* and *On Liberty*, and traces their implications for democratic politics. With the use of topical and controversial examples, including privacy, religious intolerance, and freedom of speech, he makes Mill's concerns our own at a time when what liberalism means, and why it matters, is once again in dispute.

He concludes that Mill's place in the pantheon of 'great thinkers' rests not only on his specific political and social doctrines, but above all on his steadfastly generous and liberal vision of human beings, their relations to one another, and what makes life worth living.

John Skorupski is Professor of Moral Philosophy at the University of St. Andrews. He is the author of *Symbol and Theory* (Cambridge University Press, 1976), *John Stuart Mill* (Routledge, 1989), *English Language Philosophy 1750–1945* (Oxford University Press, 1993), *Ethical Explorations* (Oxford University Press, 1999) and editor of *The Cambridge Companion to John Stuart Mill* (Cambridge University Press, 1998).

Why Read Mill Today?

John Skorupski

Routledge
Taylor & Francis Group

LONDON AND NEW YORK

First published 2006
by Routledge
2 Park Square, Milton Park, Abingdon, Oxon, OX14 4RN

Simultaneously published in the USA and Canada
by Routledge
270 Madison Ave, New York, NY 10016

First published in paperback 2007

Routledge is an imprint of the Taylor & Francis Group, an informa business

© 2006, 2007 John Skorupski

Typeset in Weiss by Taylor & Francis Books
Printed and bound in Great Britain by MPG Books Ltd, Bodmin

British Library Cataloguing in Publication Data
A catalogue record for this book is available from the British Library

Library of Congress Cataloging in Publication Data
Skorupski, John, 1946-
Why read Mill today / John Skorupski.
    p. cm.
1. Mill, John Stuart, 1806-1873. 2. Liberalism. 3. Utilitarianism.
    I. Title.
B1608.L5S56 2006
192–dc22

2005030190

ISBN10: 0-415-37744-7 (hbk)
ISBN10: 0-415-37745-5 (pbk)
ISBN10: 0-203-96871-9 (ebk)
ISBN13: 978-0-415-37744-7 (hbk)
ISBN13: 978-0-415-37745-4 (pbk)
ISBN13: 978-0-203-96871-0 (ebk)

CONTENTS

— *Contents* —

CHRONOLOGY OF MILL'S LIFE

1841	Begins correspondence with Auguste Comte.
1843	*A System of Logic, Ratiocinative and Inductive.*
1848	*Principles of Political Economy.*
1849	John Taylor dies.
1851	Marries Harriet Taylor.
1856	Becomes head of the examiners' department at India House.
1857	Indian Mutiny. Mill active in defence of the East India Company.
1858	Mill retires from the East India Company (September). Harriet dies in Avignon (November).
1859	*On Liberty.*
1861	*Utilitarianism* (published in three issues of *Fraser's Magazine*, reprinted as a book in 1863). *Considerations on Representative Government.*
1865	*An Examination of Sir William Hamilton's Philosophy.* 'Auguste Comte and Positivism'. Elected Liberal MP for Westminster.
1866	Leads public agitation to have the British Governor of Jamaica prosecuted for illegal repression of a rebellion.
1867	Unsuccessfully proposes amendment to Reform Bill to give voting rights to women.
1868	Loses seat in Parliament.
1869	*The Subjection of Women.* Writes 'Chapters on Socialism' (published in *Fortnightly Review* in 1879).
1872	Bertrand Russell born – Mill his (secular) godfather.
1873	Dies in Avignon, 7 May. Posthumous publication of *Autobiography*.

PREFACE

In comparison with other nations, the British do not seem terribly interested in their own great philosophers. They are esteemed, I think, but taken for granted. It is assumed that they have sensible, empirically-oriented and decently liberal views, and that interestingly wilder shores of philosophy are found elsewhere. Indeed, that is broadly true. But, like many things that are broadly true, this broad truth obscures other important truths. It obscures the depth and rigour of their thought, and its wide influence: in Mill's case, in particular, his significance in the development of European thought over the past two centuries. Mill was unusually receptive to the ideas that dominated the early stages of this late-modern period, and a major contributor to its later stages. As the whole period falls increasingly into perspective, some of the main land masses in the ocean of its thought stand out more clearly – I think the philosophy of Mill will emerge among them as surely as, for example, the philosophy of Hegel or Nietzsche with whom, as well as with Marx, I draw some comparisons in this book. Each of these philosophers developed new standpoints in ethics and politics that hugely influence our own state of mind: one major reason for going back to them is to expose for explicit consideration the shifting directions in our own thinking. That is especially true when our thinking is changing rather fast.

My own interest in Mill goes back a long way to my student days, and started, though it did not finish, with his moral philosophy.

I was even more interested in Marx, and through Marx, in Hegel, but there was always something about Mill's openness and straightforwardness that attracted me (it was probably what Nietzsche called his 'offensive clarity'). It has been a real pleasure to revisit those attractive Millian ideas, and to find how well – for me – they stand up to discussion, as other ideas fade. I very much hope that readers will also find it enjoyable to argue with Mill.

My thanks to my wife, Barbara, for many helpful things connected with the writing of this book.

NOTES ON THE TEXT

All citations from Mill are by volume and page number of his *Collected Works* (see Further Reading). Passages quoted from *Utilitarianism* and *On Liberty* are cited by chapter and paragraph number as well, with *U* for the former and *L* for the latter. For example, 'X: 234; *U* 4: 3' refers to volume X of the *Collected Works*, p. 234, and to *Utilitarianism* Chapter 4, paragraph 3.

Cross-references in this book are by chapter and section; thus '1.4' refers to Chapter 1, Section 4.

Quotations from Auguste Comte, G.W.F. Hegel, Friedrich Nietzsche and Karl Marx are from the following sources:

p. 19: Nietzsche, *Twilight of the Idols*, 'Maxims and Arrows' no. 13.

p. 65: Nietzsche, quoted in Stern, J. P. (1978) *Nietzsche*, London: Collins, p. 52.

p. 68: Comte, (1966) *Catéchisme Positiviste*, Paris: Garnier-Flammarion, p. 29.

p. 72: Hegel, *Philosophy of Right*, §149.

p. 75: Comte, (1875–1877) *System of Positive Polity*, vol. I, London: Longmans, Green, p. 268.

p. 80: Marx, in K. Marx and F. Engels (1975) *Collected Works*, vol. 3, New York: International Publishers. (a) 'On James Mill', p. 228, (b) The German Ideology', p. 439, (c) 'Critical Notes on the Article, "The King of Prussia and Social Reform. By a Prussian"', p. 198.

1

Free Thought

———•◆•———

Two basic questions of ethics and politics are: how should we live? And how should we live together? John Stuart Mill thought very hard about them. Still, if the questions themselves interest us, rather than the history of thought, why go back to someone who was born two hundred years ago and died in 1873? Why read him when the problems that worry us are those that face us now?

Mill provides a remarkably comprehensive liberal vision. It is complete in a way that no single thinker now could rival. There is a frankness and seriousness to it that help us to think about our own problems. Moreover, if Mill is (as I think) the wisest liberal, then not only liberals but also critics of liberalism should read him. If they are fair-minded, they should look for weaknesses in the strongest versions of liberal thought, not in weaker ones. This book is meant for both sides; it is a critical reflection, not an apologia.

Although Mill wrote about all the main questions of philosophy, this book will not discuss his philosophy as a whole. Some comprehensive studies are mentioned in the suggestions for Further Reading. Our specific concern here will be Mill's treatment of the ethical and the political questions. For this purpose, however, we do need to notice some important and distinctive features of his epistemology, in other words, his account of how we can justify our beliefs. Mill has an objective view of value that makes a thorough-going difference to his ethics and politics, and strongly distinguishes him from many twentieth-century liberals. Also relevant are his extraordinary upbringing and intellectual pedigree. So in this introductory chapter I sketch in some of the personal and philosophical background behind Mill's moral and political thought. The three chapters that follow are the main body of the book, laying out that thought. The last chapter reflects on its significance today.

1.1 Mill's life and work

Mill received his education from some of the Enlightenment's most tough-minded analysts of human nature and society. His father, James Mill, was a philosopher and historian of importance. Born on the east coast of Scotland to a poor family whose name was originally 'Milne', James progressed through Montrose Academy and then Divinity at Edinburgh University, financed by a local landowner, Sir John Stuart of Fettercairn, and his wife. He was licensed as a preacher but did not gain a living, so he moved to London and soon achieved modestly comfortable earnings in journalism. There, in 1805, he married an Englishwoman, Harriet Burrow; John Stuart Mill, his eldest son, born in 1806, was thus half-English and half-Scots. James Mill's public reputation was made by his *History of British India* (1817). It led to employment by the East India Company, of which he became a high official, eventually followed in the same post by John.

No philosopher's childhood is better known than John Stuart Mill's. He describes it, to every reader's wonder, in his *Autobiography*. He was taught by his father, beginning with Greek (at the age of 3) and arithmetic in the evenings. Before breakfast the two of them would walk out in the lanes around their home in Newington Green, then largely rural; John would report on the histories and biographies he had read the previous day. Meanwhile he studied science for his own amusement. He began on logic at the age of 12. Among James Mill's close friends were Jeremy Bentham and David Ricardo. John read Ricardo's classical *Principles of Political Economy* two years after it appeared, when he was 13. He edited Bentham's *Rationale of Judicial Evidence* – a monumental labour – when he was 18. He never went to university, but by the age of 20 he in effect had a postgraduate training in logic, political economy and jurisprudence.

In his twenties and thirties he came to know some of the most interesting younger figures in English politics and culture. His horizons broadened and his main themes were established. The *System of Logic*, the product of his thirties, published in 1843, made his reputation as a philosopher. The *Principles of Political Economy*, of 1848, was a synthesis of classical economics which defined liberal orthodoxy for at least a quarter of a century. His two best-known works of moral philosophy, *On Liberty* and *Utilitarianism*, appeared in 1859 and 1861.

A major event in his personal life was an intense – but apparently platonic – affair with a married woman, Harriet Taylor. Her intellectual and emotional influence on him has been debated by scholars ever since. She eventually became his wife in 1851, bringing them seven and a half years of great happiness before her death in 1858. In the 1860s Mill was briefly a Member of Parliament, and throughout his life was involved in many working-class and radical causes, always in a stubbornly independent way. Among them was his lifelong support for women's rights – see his essay, *The Subjection of Women* of 1869. After his election to Parliament in 1865, he presented a petition for women's suffrage in 1866, and in 1867 moved an amendment to the Reform Bill of that year, which would have extended the franchise irrespective

3

of gender; 'perhaps', he said, 'the only really important public service I performed in the capacity of a member of Parliament' (I: 285).

Mill's presence in nineteenth-century politics and culture is so powerful, his writings so diverse and detailed, that it can be hard to see his thought as a whole. Yet there is a very strong unifying theme: it is his lifelong effort to weave together the insights of the Enlightenment in which he had been reared, and the nineteenth-century reaction against it, a reaction sometimes romantic, sometimes historical and conservative, and often both. It was a dialectic that Mill experienced personally, for his childhood was an Enlightenment experiment in education, while the friends of his early manhood breathed German and Coleridgean Romanticism. An important turning point was the mental crisis and depression that afflicted him when he was 20. Its connection with his extraordinary education and claustrophobic relationship with his father is plain enough. Interesting for present purposes, though, is that it was a crisis of meaning. He asked himself whether he would be happy if all his objects in life, all the social reforms he was working for, were realised:

> And an irrepressible self-consciousness distinctly answered, 'No!' At this my heart sank within me: the whole foundation on which my life was constructed fell down ... I seemed to have nothing left to live for.
>
> (I: 139)

Now he saw the danger of too much analysis without a sufficiency of feeling; his recovery only came as feeling gradually returned. His outlook on life was very deeply affected. He retained the main structure of his Enlightenment convictions but sought to enlarge and energise it through the nineteenth-century's insight into the mutability and emotional depth and diversity of human nature. 'Many-sidedness' became his motto.

There was also a lifelong French side to Mill, through which he received influences as great as the ones already mentioned. He spoke and wrote excellent French, made a point of keeping abreast of events and ideas in France, and indeed died in France. Among many Frenchmen with whom he maintained long and productive friendships, two great figures were particularly significant: Auguste Comte, positivist and sociologist, and Alexis de Tocqueville, analyst of democracy. Mill's productive interactions with French liberalism and positivism are significant for the whole development of liberal thought. Overall, though, it is that Goethean word of power, *many-sidedness*, that best hints at what makes Mill a seminal late-modern thinker, and why fruitful comparisons can be made with Hegel, Marx and Nietzsche. 'Many-sidedness' will be one of our main themes.

1.2 Liberalism as free thought

The word 'liberal' does not refer to one single thing. Despite strong competition it must be one of the most confusing words in the political and philosophical dictionary. Indeed, one rather good reason for reassessing Mill is to get some grip on the liberal tradition, and thereby a sense of what liberalism is.

It is, among other things, a set of doctrines centring on free competition and equal opportunity. (This is the European rather than the current American sense of the word, but it is the one that is more historical.) Mill, as one of the nineteenth century's leading economists, wrote plenty on these subjects, giving liberalism in the economic sphere a definite and principled shape; at the same time he also had much to say about social justice, favouring strongly redistributive measures, and experiments with workers' co-operatives. More fundamentally – and rather separately – liberalism is a moral doctrine limiting the authority of state and society over individuals. This is the most famous aspect of Mill's liberalism; his essay *On Liberty* sets out a highly influential limiting doctrine of this kind. More fundamentally still, liberalism can be thought of as a vision of how to live, what human good is, and how our mutual relations should be regulated. Here Mill stands out as a talismanic, though controversial, liberal presence. The political philosopher John Rawls called this kind of overall vision 'comprehensive liberalism', citing Mill and Kant as its two great, though distinct, examples.

We can dig even deeper. We can go right back to the sources of liberalism in the modern West by considering the purely philosophical idea of free thought – *libre pensée*. Liberalism, at bottom, is simply free thought, and Kant and Mill are both liberals in this deepest way. For both of them the ideal of free thought is the most fundamental liberal ideal.

Free thought is thought ruled by its own principles and by nothing else; in other words, by principles of thinking that it discovers by reflecting on its own activity. It acknowledges no external constraints placed on it by doctrines of faith, revelation or received authority: it scrutinises such teachings in the light of its own principles. One can also say that free thought is thought ruled solely by natural reason, if 'natural reason' is just a name for all those principles that are internal to thinking and reflectively acknowledged by it as its own. The contrast is with *apologetic* thought, in the traditional and respectable sense of that word – thought which seeks to make intelligible, so far as possible, the ways of God to man, without claiming to know those ways by its own principles alone. The apologetic tradition is fideistic, in the sense that it holds that free thought alone cannot tell us what to believe. Natural reason must be a servant of faith, or at best a co-sovereign with it.

The liberal question of freedom and authority, of what I must determine for myself and what I must accept from other sources, begins right here. Free thought, and with it liberty of discussion, are fundamental to Mill's philosophy.

But now we reach an important fork in the road. Down one route lies the idea of free thought as thought that is *unconstrained* by any authoritative source external to it. Down the other lies the idea of it as radically *presuppositionless*. It is basic to Mill's stance in epistemology that he takes free thought to be necessarily the former but necessarily not the latter. There are, he emphasises, no constraints on free thought, but that does not mean it can start from nowhere.

Yet the idea that free thought must be presuppositionless is highly plausible. If it rests on some presupposition or assumption, how can it be free? Must it not freely question that assumption? That has been an enormously influential modern conception of what it is to think really freely. Call it the Cartesian idea, after the French philosopher, René Descartes, who expounded it in his *Meditations*. Descartes allows all our opinions to be questioned by the radical sceptic and then tries to find a refutation of the sceptic that relies on none of those opinions but only on itself – that is, on the mere fact of thinking. One can say without exaggeration that this project of defeating the sceptic on his own terms without any presupposition – together with its complete failure – is one of the main shapers of modernity. And this means that it has made a big difference to the fortunes of liberalism.

One way of spelling out its shaping influence would be to tell the story of German philosophy from Kant to Nietzsche. This tradition takes the Cartesian idea with utmost seriousness, and then seriously tries to free itself from its clutch. Kant responds to Descartes' failure by a critique of free thought itself (the 'Critique of Pure Reason'). Truly free thought, he says, must investigate the conditions of its own possibility. It turns out that those conditions take human beings out of the world: as *free* thinkers and agents they are not a part of nature, but have a noumenal aspect. The story continues with Hegel. He finds fault with Kant's project because it imposes a basic cleavage of subject and object. So he tries to show how free thought itself literally generates every-thing: a kind of apotheosis of presuppositionless free thought. Nietzsche sees the failure of these high-wire heroics and diag-noses a crisis of Western values.

The deep and genuine difficulty is to see how free thought can be both self-authorising *and* truth-finding, in the way the modern outlook assumes. Nietzsche thinks it cannot be: we must give up on truth and recognise that we impose our own 'values'. That Nietzschean idea, so liberating and counter-cultural in its day, went on to influence high modernism and eventually to become a popular dogma of our time. Epistemology has entered politics in a big way, in that sceptical or subjectivist attitudes have become basic to our ethical and political outlook – the very outlook about which Nietzsche was so scathing. It is an undercurrent that sig-nificantly distinguishes Mill's and Nietzsche's respective attitudes to democracy and equality (see Chapter 5).

1.3 *Thinking from within*

Mill belongs to the alternative tradition, according to which free thought does not start by refusing to make any assumptions at all, but instead maintains a continuing critical open-mindedness about everything we take ourselves to know, without any exemptions whatever. This 'constructive empiricism' also goes back to the seventeenth century. It is naturalistic, in that it takes us to be a part of the world that we scientifically study. It is holistic, in that it works from within our convictions as a whole. It takes the fal-libilist attitude that *any* of the things we think we know, however seemingly certain, could turn out to be wrong in the course of our continuing inquiry. That includes our initial assumptions – but it does not follow that we cannot start from them.

Mill's constructive empiricism is one main way in which he maintains a firm footing in the Enlightenment. He is unimpressed by 'the well-meant but impracticable precept of Descartes' of 'setting out from the supposition that nothing had been already ascertained' (VII: 318–19). That way lies only nihilism, for nothing can come of nothing. Nor does he think that an *a priori* critique can show us that human beings as thinkers have some non-natural noumenal side. Thinking is itself a natural process:

> Principles of Evidence and Theories of Method are not to be constructed *a priori*. The laws of our rational faculty, like those of every other natural agency, are only learnt by seeing the agent at work ... we should never have known by what process truth is to be ascertained, if we had not previously ascertained many truths.
>
> (VIII: 833)

It is in this way that free thought discovers truths about what we should believe, about what is good, about how we should act – truths that are normative for our thinking, feeling and doing. It does so by careful scrutiny of how we actually reason and reflective analysis of which principles in this practice of reasoning turn out to be treated by us as normatively basic: 'seeing the agent at work'. This is the only 'evidence' that can be produced for the philosopher's normative claims.

I will call this method 'thinking from within'. (Hegel's method, incidentally, could also be described as thinking from within: this is one of surprisingly many common points that can be found between the two very different thinkers, and it contributes a liberal aspect to Hegel's thinking.) Thinking from within requires imaginative understanding of other people and other times; a lesson Mill drew from Coleridge. About other people's ideas, Mill says, Bentham's only question was, were they true? Coleridge, in contrast, patiently asked after their meaning. To pin down the fundamental norms of our thinking calls for careful psychological and historical inquiry into how people think, and also into how they think they should think – what kind of normative attitudes they display in their actions and their reflection. These must be engaged with to be understood. So thinking from within is inherently dialogical. And it always remains corrigible. Both points are significant in Mill's argument for liberty of thought and discussion.

What gives this method a critical and systematic edge? It can examine whether some normative dispositions are reducible to other such dispositions. It can also consider whether some are explicable in a way that subverts their authority. Suppose I can explain your low opinion of your brother's intelligence as the product solely of sheer envy and resentment. That will subvert this opinion: it may be true, but your grounds for thinking it is are not good ones. Or an example Mill would have liked: normative notions of what women's role should be may simply reflect unequal power relationships between men and women. That, if true, subverts these normative views. It does not show they are false but it does show that they are not justified. Thinking from within seeks to establish what basic normative dispositions are not subvertible in this way, but are *resilient* under reflection and thus preserve normative authority.

Mill never tries to justify this approach against the heroic presuppositionless tradition. Is this wise avoidance of an ultimately pointless question, or unacceptable evasion of a fundamental question? Religious fideists, on the one hand, and post-modern nihilists on the other, will answer that it is the latter. They have a point. To say that thinking from within is the method we actually use in our best philosophising, and the only method we could use, still does not answer the Kantian question, which asks what *right* we have to use it. How, to repeat, can free thought be both self-authorising *and* truth-finding? Mill's reply would be that free thought has the only vindication it can have: its own success in practice, as shown by its history. On its own record it does not lead to disaster but to the growth of knowledge and to an outlook that is humanistic and liberal.

But because the sceptical fall-out from the other, pre-suppositionless, tradition has become so culturally influential, it is now an important question not just for pure philosophy, but for ethics and politics, whether Mill's confidence in the process of fallible dialogue is legitimate. A strange alliance of religious apologists and 'post-modern' nihilists disagrees. Do they not need to be confronted directly? Isn't ignoring them and just getting on with it a bit smug? Alas – this question can be put briefly but can be discussed only at subtle length. Much philosophy remains concerned with it. The fact is, however, that it is not a discussion that suited Mill. He is patient in understanding other people's substantive outlooks, but impatient of elusive meta-discussions. Even so, he remains indispensable to those who trust in free thought and discussion, because he shows what thinking open-mindedly, with integrity, can achieve.

1.4 *Religion*

The question of free thought, and of understanding other people's outlooks, leads one to consider Mill's attitude to religion. He tells us in his *Autobiography* that he is one of the few examples in Britain 'of one who has, not thrown off belief, but never had it' (I: 45). Religion is absent from his philosophy, in the sense that working out a metaphysics in which God and immortality have a fundamental place is simply not something he needs to do. But it is not absent as a meaning-giving human belief and, especially, as a way of life; these aspects of religion always interested him.

When in a late essay he discusses 'Theism', he does so within the epistemological framework I have described, that is, purely from the standpoint of natural reason. He treats the existence of

God as a hypothesis to be assessed on empirical grounds. The best empirical evidence for it, he thinks, is the existence of organisms that could be explained as products of intelligent design. Such evidence does give some ground, 'insufficient for proof, and amounting only to one of the lower degrees of probability' (X: 482), for postulating an intelligent designer. The kind of designer it points to is not an eternal omnipotent intelligence that created the whole universe, but rather an intelligence limited by the natural materials and laws with which it had to work. Mill adds that Darwin's theory of evolution would further decrease the probability of this hypothesis, since it would explain how complex functional systems such as the eye could emerge without forethought by a designer. He was enthusiastic about Darwin's 'remarkable speculation', but reserved judgement as to whether it would be finally accepted ('Theism' was written about ten years after the publication of *The Origin of Species* in 1859).

In any case, he is firm that the 'notion of a providential government by an omnipotent Being for the good of his creatures must be entirely dismissed' (X: 482). In view of the existence of evil, perfect goodness in the intelligent designer cannot be reconciled with perfect power: 'The attempt to do so not only involves absolute contradiction in an intellectual point of view but exhibits to excess the revolting spectacle of a jesuitical defence of moral enormities' (X: 456).

The first point is too strong, in that the existence of evil does not positively contradict what the apologist must believe, namely, that the world we live in belongs to the best possible set of worlds. But Mill could have said that there is no evidence at all for that belief. Elsewhere, he considers a still popular obfuscatory line, according to which not just God's purposes but the very meaning of His goodness must be a mystery to us, because the finite goodness of human beings provides no model for the infinite goodness of God. It rouses Mill to his much-quoted reply:

I will call no being good, who is not what I mean when I apply that epithet to my fellow-creatures; and if such a being can sentence me to hell for not so calling him, to hell I will go.

(IX: 103)

The defiant tone is slightly comic, but the point made follows directly from the liberal attitude of free thought. The only understanding we have of 'good' is that given by our own standards of goodness. Faith has no authority to tell us that 'infinite goodness' refers to something that we cannot understand, but must believe, without understanding, to deserve the highest veneration.

And yet Mill wants to leave some space for religious hope. That there exists a powerful though not omnipotent being who wishes us well, and may somehow offer us the prospect of life after death, is a possibility that need not be dismissed. We do not have sufficient grounds to believe it, but we do have sufficient grounds for legitimate hope, and such a hope may comfort and inspire. This striking conclusion has made some people think that Mill had a wistful desire to believe after all. That is a misconception. He simply provides an assessment of the very best that can be said for religion, in the spirit of a fair-minded but detached philosopher's review. He gives a similarly fair-minded account of the good and bad consequences of religious faith, in the companion essay, 'The Utility of Religion'. There is no evidence that he himself hoped. Once the theory of evolution became well established, he would probably have felt compelled to say that even the margin for hope had gone.

What *is* true is that Mill's nature needed a great ideal, something 'grander and more beautiful than we see realized in the prose of human life' (X: 419). It was this that had precipitated his mental crisis. Mill thought that religion, in its highest poetic

13

forms, supplied one such ideal. And it could make one love goodness. He saw that clearly, but also saw that these were not in themselves reasons to believe it. He was moved by other, humanistic, ideals. There is above all what I shall call the liberal ideal (2.3), but there is also an ideal of working with others for a common good, and an ideal of service to humanity, which makes him sympathise with Comte's 'religion of humanity' even as he finds its details absurd and rejects its liberticidal aspects. In the end, the test of ideals for Mill – after his mental crisis as before it – is how much they contribute to human happiness. Which leads on to our next chapter.

2

The Good for Human Beings

———•◆•———

2.1 Happiness and self-development

What is the good for human beings? Mill thinks that it consists in happiness. He means pleasure or enjoyment and the absence of suffering. Only happiness contributes to making the world a better or worse place. No-one's happiness is more important than anyone else's, so the happiness of all must be the sole ultimate standard of what ends are worth pursuing and what things worth doing. This is 'the greatest happiness principle', the fundamental principle determining how good any end or objective is. It is what Mill means by 'utilitarianism'.

It might seem, given this view, that we must devote all our energies to making the world a happier place. Yet that is emphatically not what Mill thinks. Selfless pursuit of the general happiness, if it is well done, is admirable, but it is not the general rule. The general rule, Mill thinks, should be that everyone pursues their own happiness in their own way, under the limitations set by the equal rights of everyone else. And even when it comes to pursuing one's own happiness, for most people that is best done by pursuing other ends and achieving happiness by the way. Happiness 'is the justification, and ought to be the controller, of all ends, but is not itself the sole end' (VIII: 952).

The reasons for this have to do with some basic truths about what human beings are like, their history, and their shared situation. They best discover their own forms of happiness by making their own mistakes; they discover happiness by and large at least as much in their own personal spheres of self, family and friends as in the impersonal sphere of ethical or political activism; above all, for human beings, the most cherishable forms of happiness require personal freedom, the freedom to get on with one's own life in one's own way. Some of Mill's most splendid outbursts are aimed at moralists who want to *impose* service to mankind as the rule of life:

> Why is it necessary that all human life should point but to one object, and be cultivated into a system of means to a single end? May it not be the fact that mankind, who after all are made up of single human beings, obtain a greater sum of happiness when each pursues his own, under the rules and conditions required by the good of the rest, than when each makes the good of the rest his only object, and allows himself no personal pleasures not indispensable to the preservation of his faculties? The regimen of a blockaded town should be cheerfully submitted to when high purposes require it, but is it the ideal perfection of human existence?
>
> (X: 337)

This is directed against Auguste Comte. Mill was very ready to admire the ideal of working for human good – and responded to it personally to a quite unusual degree. Yet he thought Comte a 'morality-intoxicated man', and in politics, a 'liberticide'. The morality-intoxication and the liberticide are connected. If everyone's sole duty is to live for the good of others (*'vivre pour autrui'*), then why not have a state in which that duty is enforced? The disaster lies in making the admirable obligatory:

There is a standard of altruism to which all should be required to come up, and a degree beyond which it is not obligatory, but meritorious. It is incumbent on every one to restrain the pursuit of his personal objects within the limits consistent with the essential interests of others. What those limits are, it is the province of ethical science to determine; and to keep all individuals and aggregates of individuals within them, is the proper office of punishment and of moral blame. If in addition to fulfilling this obligation, persons make the good of others a direct object of disinterested exertions, postponing or sacrificing to it even innocent personal indulgences, they deserve gratitude and honour, and are fit objects of moral praise. So long as they are in no way compelled to this conduct by any external pressure, there cannot be too much of it; but a necessary condition is its spontaneity; since the notion of a happiness for all, procured by the self-sacrifice of each, if the abnegation is really felt to be a sacrifice, is a contradiction.

(X: 337–8)

The distinctions that are made in these passages are basic to Mill's kind of liberalism. He does not ground liberal principles on a doctrine of natural rights of person and property, as Locke does; nor on rights supposed to apply to all rational beings, as Kant does; nor does he derive the state from a social contract, as they do. His case is empirically based on actual human nature. The institutions of the liberal state, Mill thinks, are those under which human beings are happiest. Other sorts of beings might flourish under quite different institutions. But human beings need liberty, and they find that in a social order that leaves them to pursue their 'personal objects within the limits consistent with the essential interests of others'. The next chapter will examine what Mill thinks those limits are.

Mill has a specific view about why human beings need liberty to be happy. It is because they can develop themselves only when they are free, and because self-development is a condition of the highest forms of happiness. Happiness of this kind is achieved through living by some objectively sound ideal. The altruistic ideal, of living for others, is certainly *one* of these; when embraced freely, it can be a great source of self-realising happiness. But it cannot be imposed as a moral obligation, since a 'necessary condition is its spontaneity'. And importantly, as we shall see, it is only one of many admirable ideals, and can be a main avenue of self-realising happiness only for some.

The notion of self-development, and its connection with ideals of living, is crucial for Mill. It forms part of an overall argument connecting happiness and freedom. In this chapter we shall examine its structural foundations: the Greatest Happiness Principle, how Mill tries to establish it, and how he thinks ideals of living are connected to happiness.

2.2 *The Greatest Happiness Principle*

Mill's foundational principle breaks down into a number of subclaims. There is the question of what is good for human beings. There is the question of why the general good, the good of all, should be the ultimate criterion of conduct – why shouldn't the ultimate criterion be the good of the person who is deliberating about what to do? And then, even if the general good of all is the criterion, why should we represent the general good as the *sum* of the good of each? Mill is at his best in answering the first question. He is quite perfunctory in answering the other two.

To ask what is ultimately good, he says, is to ask what ends are ultimately desirable; and 'the sole evidence it is possible to produce that anything is desirable, is that people do actually desire it' (X: 234; *U* 4: 3). Or as he also puts it, that it is desired 'in theory and practice'. In other words the 'evidence' for its being desirable is simply that when we reflect on what we desire, we find that we desire this (whatever it may be) for itself, and acknowledge it as indeed desirable – rather than subverting that judgement and trying to change our desires. This must indeed be the basic test for any normative claim, according to the method of inquiry I called 'thinking from within' (1.3). And by this test, according to Mill, happiness, understood as 'pleasure, and the absence of pain' (X: 210; *U* 2: 2), emerges as an ultimately desirable end.

So far, so good. Few deny in theory, let alone in practice, that pleasure is desirable. There are some: 'Man does *not* strive for pleasure', according to Nietzsche, 'only the Englishman does.' It is not one of his more convincing propositions. A much more formidable question is whether happiness is the *only* ultimately desirable thing. Mill thinks it is; he is, in other words, a 'hedonist'. So by his own method he has to show that happiness is the only thing ultimately desired. That in turn is 'a question of fact and experience' which 'can only be determined by practised self-consciousness and self-observation, assisted by observation of others' (X: 237; *U* 4:10). Such observation shows, he thinks, that when we want something for its own sake and with no further end in view, we want it because we think of it as enjoyable, or think of not having it as positively painful. He regards this as a psychological law about all desires.

It does not mean, however, that we desire all objects as *means* to our pleasure. The desire for an object is genuinely a desire for that object; it is not the desire for pleasure as such. Mill's way of marking this is to say that the object is desired as a 'part' of one's happiness. So the claim that happiness is the sole human end, put more carefully, is this: 'Whatever is desired otherwise than as a means to some end beyond itself, and ultimately to happiness, is desired as itself a part of happiness, and is not desired for itself until has become so' (X: 237; *U* 4: 8). Pluralists about human ends deny that. They hold that there are desirable ends other than happiness. So if they follow Mill's method they must deny the thesis that whatever we desire, we desire under the idea of it as pleasant. They can say that desiring something does always involve the idea of it as worth doing or bringing about, but does *not* always involve the idea that the doing or achieving of it will be pleasant (or pain-avoiding).

Thus, for example, I may want to know that I have a terminal illness if I do. I think of that knowledge as something worth having, but not necessarily as something I would enjoy having. Again, I love others and I am committed to causes; I want these others and these causes to flourish, even though I don't necessarily expect to be around to enjoy it. A third example: I want to be able to get on with things in my own way, and not have people, including well-intentioned people, interfering. On the basis of such examples, the pluralist argues against Mill that for many people things such as knowledge of one's situation, the good of people and causes with which one identifies, and freedom to live one's life in one's own way are reflectively desired, hence desirable, in just as ultimate a way as pleasure.

Mill's response will be to acknowledge that knowledge, the well-being of people one cares for, personal independence, and so on, are indeed desired for themselves. What that means, however, is that they are desired as parts rather than as means to happiness. That is what he says, for example, about the desire to be a virtuous person. Good people desire virtue for itself: in other words, Mill says, they desire it as part of their happiness and are unhappy if they are aware of lacking it. However, while the distinction between desiring something as a means to happiness and as a part of it is well taken, it does not settle the issue. A pluralist will reply that we are ready and willing to give up some happiness *overall* to further certain other ends that we have; not out of a sense of obligation to pursue them but just because we want to pursue them. You want to know if you have cancer even if that knowledge will produce some net reduction in your happiness. Is that an unreasonable want?

This debate between hedonist and pluralist can be pursued with care and in detail. It is important not only for the personal question of how one should live, but also, given Mill's framework, as a question about what human ends serve as foundations of liberalism. Although hedonism has strong and subtle resources, it seems to me that the pluralist is right. And it's interesting that Mill himself says things that are only reconcilable with hedonism by means of a little pushing and shoving, for example, when at one point he contrasts the 'comparatively humble sense' of happiness, as 'pleasure and freedom from pain', with the 'higher meaning', namely, what 'human beings with highly developed faculties can care to have' (VIII: 952). I don't think such passages show he is not a hedonist, when everything else he says is taken into account, but they do show the strain between two elements in his thinking.

We can ask a person, 'How good are you feeling right now? How much are you enjoying what you're doing?' We can also ask, 'How satisfied are you with your life? Is it the life you "care to have"? How well are things going for you overall?' These are very different kinds of questions (as psychological research on happiness bears out). According to hedonism, how well things are going for you *overall* should be measured by how high you are scoring over time in answer to the first question. But that's not what many people think. Mill is right to analyse a person's good as what is desirable for that person. But what a person may reasonably desire can extend beyond his own enjoyment into outcomes he cannot even know. So if my good is what is desirable for me, as Mill thinks, my good extends likewise.

Let's turn to the other two questions I mentioned above. They arise whether one takes a hedonist or a pluralist view of human good. Why should the general good, the good of all, be the ultimate criterion of conduct, rather than each particular person's good being the ultimate criterion for that particular person? And even if the general good of all is the criterion, why should we represent the general good as the sum of the good of each?

Mill never adequately examined these elements in the principle of utility. When he states the utilitarian doctrine before considering what kind of proof can be given of it, he states it thus: 'happiness is desirable, and the only thing desirable, as an end, all other things being only desirable as means to that end' (X: 234; *U* 4: 2). Evidently he thinks that the controversial part of his task is to show that this – i.e. hedonism – is true. All he has to say about the further move from hedonism to the utility principle is that if 'each person's happiness is a good to that person', then 'the general happiness' must be 'a good to the aggregate of all persons' (X: 234; *U* 4: 3). In a letter in which he explains this unclear remark, he says: 'I merely meant in this particular sentence to argue that since A's happiness is a good, B's a good, C's a good, etc, the sum of all these goods must be a good' (XVI: 1414).

But this clarification makes two assumptions. First, even if Mill has shown that each person's happiness is a good *to that person*, a philosophical egoist can still deny that he has shown that happiness is a good. There is no such thing as the good *period*, the egoist says; there's only what's good *for you* or *for me*. Against the egoist Mill needs a postulate of impartiality, and a corresponding natural disposition. We must be naturally disposed to hold that everyone's good is of legitimate concern to all of us, and that no-one's well-being is in this respect more important than anyone else's.

The second assumption is more subtle. At the end of the last chapter of *Utilitarianism*, 'On the Connexion between Justice and Utility', Mill does explain that he takes 'perfect impartiality between persons' to be part of the very meaning of the Greatest

Happiness Principle: 'That principle is a mere form of words without rational signification, unless one person's happiness, supposed equal in degree (with the proper allowance made for kind), is counted for exactly as much as another's' (X: 257; *U* 5: 36). So here Mill supplies the required postulate of impartiality. However, the concept of impartiality does not, taken on its own, yield utilitarianism's aggregative principle of distribution. Maximising the sum of individuals' happiness, if it makes sense to talk in this way at all, is but one way of being impartial. It is not the only one. A wide variety of non-equivalent distributive principles is impartial in the sense that they do not count any one person's happiness as more important than anyone else's. The most that can be gained from combining a postulate of impartiality with hedonism is a generic thesis: that the general good is some positive impartial function of the happiness of all individuals and of nothing else. What Mill needed to argue, to support his specific view, was that we are naturally disposed to take the *sum* of individuals' happiness rather than to apply some other impartial criterion.

As a psychological hypothesis, that looks implausible. Suppose, for example, that we are considering a world in which everyone lives in reasonable comfort. In these circumstances, I suspect, very few people would regard a smallish increase in sum-total well-being achieved at the cost of serious suffering for a small number of people to be an *improvement*. To say that is to gesture at highly difficult issues, about what plausible distributive constraints should be placed on the structure of impartially conceived good (and how determinate an answer can be given) – issues that have come to the fore since Mill wrote.

If faced with these issues, how strongly would Mill have wanted to defend the sum-total view? I believe that his fundamental commitment is simply that the general good, impartially conceived, is the ultimate criterion of conduct. He could retreat from the sum-total view of general good to a view which gave it a more constrained distributive structure, and there seems to be no particular theoretical reason why he should not do so.

Hedonism has deeper roots in his overall philosophy, despite his tendency to veer away from it from time to time. Suppose, however, we accept that human beings have ultimate ends other than happiness. I've mentioned knowledge of one's situation, freedom to do things one's own way, the good of people and causes that one has come to identify with as one's own. The result of these two changes (away from the sum-total version of impartiality, and away from hedonism) would still be a species of an important general position, though a more complex one: namely, that the good is the well-being of all, impartially considered. Call this generic position 'philosophical utilitarianism'. And the more complex version of philosophical utilitarianism is arguably more favourable to Mill's kind of liberalism than his own version of it is.

It could still be defended in Mill's way, by thinking from within, focusing on what is found, by an empirical inquiry into our sentiments, to be what human beings in fact desire. But what about the requirement of impartiality itself? How do we defend that? Without it, Mill's structure falls apart. I will come back to this crucial question in 5.3.

A final point. Philosophical utilitarianism holds that it is not just human beings, but all beings capable of well-being, that count. This plainly leads to important questions about the moral status of non-human animals, of which Mill is well aware. Nonetheless he has little to say about them, even if he should have had more. And since our focus here is on Mill as a philosopher of liberalism, I shall not pursue them. I turn instead to his liberal ideal.

2.3 *The liberal ideal*

Utility – general well-being impartially conceived – is Mill's ethical foundation; it must therefore be the foundation of his liberalism. So in the essay *On Liberty*, Mill duly says that his argument does not rest on 'the idea of abstract right, as a thing independent of utility', but that he regards utility as 'the ultimate appeal on all ethical questions' (XVIII: 224; L 1: 11).

He immediately adds that the utility in question must be utility 'in the largest sense, grounded on the permanent interests of man as a progressive being'. It is a significant phrase. These 'permanent interests' arise from human beings' potential for free self-development, and that is a potential realised not only in the course of individual lives but progressively in human history itself.

No point is more fundamental for grasping Mill's ethical and political outlook. Its essence is a conception of human good as something dynamic, developmental and individual. Human beings can raise or lower themselves: they can develop their good towards the higher or the lower. They have it in themselves to take charge. Mill thinks that that capacity to develop oneself in one's own way – culture of the self by the self – is present in us all. We are potentially self-forming, developmental, in a way that other animals are not. Yet he also thinks that societies in which universal free self-culture becomes truly possible come about only through a long historical development. When that stage is reached, self-development becomes the proper task of human beings. People then have to do their own work of self-development, because human potentialities are diverse and best known to the individual person, and because only by working out their own plans of life do they develop moral freedom. Self-development always contains possibilities of regression as well as progress, but good social institutions enable free self-development to flourish and go on flourishing, without stagnating or regressing.

This progressive and developmental notion of the human good was widely held in nineteenth-century culture. The idealist side of the debate called it 'self-realisation', but it was not only idealists who held it. What was controversial was what the content of self-realisation would be. There were conflicting ideals of self-realisation; we have seen, for example, Comte's altruistic ideal. For Mill, the content of self-realisation was given by a certain liberal ideal of character.

An important source for it is the aesthetic and ethical vision of classical Greek (specifically Athenian) life that was presented by German thinkers and artists at the turn of the eighteenth century. It was an ideal of balanced development of all faculties – rational self-governance on the one hand and development and education of the feelings, 'aesthetic education', on the other: 'a Greek ideal of self-development, which the Platonic and Christian ideal of self-government blends with, but does not supersede' (XVIII: 266; L 3: 8).

This ideal is the nineteenth century's most important contribution to liberal ethics. It transforms the philosophical liberalism of that time from the liberalisms that came before. We might call it the 'neo-Greek', 'neo-Renaissance' or 'humanistic' ideal, to indicate that it belongs to a particular epoch in the liberal tradition and is not definitive of every kind of liberal politics. The point is well taken; but since in a book on Mill this ideal inevitably crops up all the time, and since it seems to me to be connected with such notions as 'liberal education', I will simply call it for short 'the liberal ideal'.

How does Mill reconcile such an ideal of active and high-minded self-culture with his theory of happiness as the only good, with its tough-minded, seemingly low and passive-sounding insistence on 'pleasure and the absence of pain?' He sees no contradiction. These low and passive associations are the spin of utilitarianism's indefatigable opponents. When Mill considers the accusation that the Greatest Happiness Principle is a philosophy for swine, he answers that the objection assumes human beings have no pleasures other than those of swine. The question that interests him is what *human* happiness consists in, and how it can be achieved in the world as it is. He returns to these questions throughout his writings, again and again.

The liberal ideal of self-culture is perfectly compatible with the greatest happiness principle. For only through free self-culture, subject to the rules required by the interests of all, is the fullest self-development achieved. And the crucial link that then links self-development with happiness is the following: only the fullest self-development of one's potential gives access to the highest forms of human happiness. The political philosopher John Rawls called this idea 'the Aristotelian principle', citing both Aristotle's *Nicomachean Ethics* and Mill's *Utilitarianism*. The similarity is well noticed. It is likely, however, that Mill was influenced by 'Germano-Coleridgean' ideas, as he called them, rather than by Aristotle – he thought Aristotle lacked the historical and progressive conception of human well-being which was to him, Mill, so important (XI: 505). Certainly he develops the idea in his own way, and since it is so fundamental to his ethics and politics I will call it the *Millian principle*.

In his *Autobiography*, he dates two new convictions to his recovery from a period of depression that assailed him in 1826–27 (when he was 20). He still thought that happiness alone is the true end of life. But he now thought that 'this end was only to be attained by not making it the direct end' (I: 145), an important theme that we have already noticed. Second, he now

> gave its proper place, among the prime necessities of human well-being, to the internal culture of the individual ... The maintenance of a due balance among the faculties now seemed to me to be of primary importance. The cultivation of the feelings became one of the cardinal points in my ethical and philosophical creed.
>
> (I: 147)

The accent Mill places here and elsewhere on 'cultivation of the feelings' arises because of what he thought he had to combat: an over-emphasis on development of reason and will represented by the 'Platonic and Christian ideal of self-government', a one-sidedness that had shown itself in the deficiencies of his own upbringing, and more importantly, dominated the new bourgeois culture's notion of respectability. It is not that he thinks it wrong to emphasise the development of reason and will; the point is that it becomes a distorting emphasis if it is not combined with insight into the education of the feelings. Liberal education is about 'due balance'. Friedrich Schiller, the German poet and philosopher, had made exactly the same criticism of Kant's moral philosophy. He thought Kant had given an inspiring account of one side of human nature: its 'dignity'. But he had not captured humanity's 'grace' – its spontaneity of feeling. Schiller's *Letters on the Aesthetic Education of Man* are a seminal contribution to the liberal ideal; this was an element in the German Romantic ferment of the time to which Mill was especially open (though his own openness to feeling had come as much from poetry, especially Wordsworth's poetry, as from German philosophical Romanticism).

Reason and will are required for (and nurtured by) free discussion, civic participation, and the active direction of one's life. Mill calls this quality of rational will 'moral freedom', and like Kant, identifies it with reliable virtue:

> A person feels morally free who feels that his habits or his temptations are not his masters, but he theirs: who even in yielding to them knows that he could resist … we must feel that our wish, if not strong enough to alter our character, is strong enough to conquer our character when the two are brought into conflict in any particular case of conduct. And hence it is said with truth, that none but a person of confirmed virtue is completely free.
>
> (VIII: 841)

He worried about whether moral freedom was compatible with his naturalistic view of human beings, but thought he saw how they could be reconciled (in the *System of Logic* – Book 6, Chapter 2 – from which I have just quoted, and which Mill thought the best chapter in the whole work).

What we do, he said, is always causally explicable by a motive, but that motive need not be a desire: 'A habit of willing is commonly called a purpose; and among the causes of our volitions, and of the actions which flow from them, must be reckoned not only likings and aversions, but also purposes' (VIII: 842). Will evolves through the psychological differentiation of purposes from desires: when it has evolved we can act purposively against our desires. That is essential to Mill's conception of character, as in *Utilitarianism*, where we find him insisting 'positively and emphatically':

> that the will is a different thing from desire; that a person of confirmed virtue, or any other person whose purposes are fixed, carries out his purposes without any thought of the pleasure he has in contemplating them, or expects to derive from their fulfilment.
>
> (X: 238; *U* 4: 11)

Sir Thomas Bertram, in Jane Austen's *Mansfield Park*, would applaud. And so would Immanuel Kant. But the 'virtuous will' is not for Mill an intrinsic good, as it is for Kant. It remains:

> a means to good, not intrinsically a good; and does not contradict the doctrine that nothing is good to human beings but in so far as it is either itself pleasurable, or a means of attaining pleasure or averting pain.
>
> (X: 239; *U* 4:11)

It does not contradict the doctrine, because the criterion of what is good or desirable as a final end remains what we *desire*, not what we will.

So Mill accepts the existence and importance of the developed will, and its connection with right character – the human characteristic Schiller called 'dignity'. Yet at the same time he thinks that virtue belongs to the feelings as well: because it is loveable and desirable it can come to be loved and desired for itself. Then it becomes a part of our happiness – Schiller's 'grace' – and of course Mill thinks it a good thing that it should be so.

Character itself involves strongly developed feeling as well as strongly developed will:

> A person whose desires and impulses are his own – are the expression of his own nature, as it has been developed and modified by his own culture – is said to have a character. One whose desires and impulses are not his own, has no character, no more than a steam engine has character.
>
> (XVIII: 264; *L* 3: 5)

What is it for desires and impulses to be one's own? The key notion here is that of spontaneity, in a traditional philosophical sense in which a spontaneous volition or action is one that flows directly from one's own nature. Likewise with spontaneous feeling: it flows directly from one's nature, in other words it is not factitious, uncritically accepted from without, unthinkingly conventional, the product merely of a wish to please or to conform. This idea is linked to education or culture, as against indoctrination: education brings out and develops our spontaneous responses, whether these be cognitive, conative or affective, in accordance with their own immanent rationality. Thus virtue can be spontaneously loved for itself because it *is* loveable, whereas wealth cannot be *spontaneously* loved for *itself*. Immanent rationality is related to the idea of thinking from within: it is what naturally strikes us, from within the standpoint of feeling, as reasonable, fitting, normatively apt in itself. All human value is founded on this immanent rationality of the feelings, and can be founded in no other way. Educating the feelings consists in developing them in accordance with their spontaneity. The process is inherently dialogical and exploratory, and can take place fully only under conditions of freedom.

It is not surprising then that 'free development of individuality' and 'individual spontaneity' are key notions for Mill. It is what he opposes to his age's 'narrow theory of life, and to the pinched and hidebound type of human character which it patronizes' (XVIII: 265; L 3: 8):

> There is a different type of human excellence from the Calvinistic: a conception of humanity as having its nature bestowed on it for other purposes than merely to be abnegated. 'Pagan self-assertion' is one of the elements of human worth, as well as 'Christian self-denial'. There is a Greek ideal of self-development, which the Platonic and Christian ideal of self-government blends with, but does not supersede. It may be better to be a John Knox than an Alcibiades, but it is better to be a Pericles than either; nor would a Pericles, if we had one in these days, be without anything good which belonged to John Knox.
>
> (XVIII: 265–6; L 3: 8)

2.4 Qualities of happiness

That there is such a thing as education of the feelings is the foundation of Mill's famous distinction between quality and quantity of pleasure:

It is quite compatible with the principle of utility, to recognise the fact that some *kinds* of pleasure are more desirable and more valuable than others. It would be absurd that while, in estimating all other things, quality is considered as well as quantity, the estimation of pleasures should be supposed to depend on quantity alone.

(X: 211; *U* 2: 4)

Once again that works through the Millian principle: the point is that developed human beings acquire capacities for enjoyment that undeveloped human beings lack. These are the pleasures of higher quality – the ones that 'human beings with highly developed faculties can care to have'.

The charge has often been made that this supposed distinction between quality and quantity of pleasure is actually inconsistent with hedonism. Not so. There is no reason in logic why more than one characteristic of pleasures should not be relevant to estimating their value; though if we call those characteristics 'quantity' and 'quality', we need to maintain a careful distinction between the quantity and quality of a pleasure on the one hand and its degree of value on the other (as Mill does in the passage just cited). Activity A can be more valuable pleasure-wise than activity B, because though it gives less pleasure, the pleasure it gives is of higher quality. All that hedonism requires is that the only things that make a pleasure valuable are its characteristics as a *pleasure*.

How then do we know the qualities of pleasures? According to Mill, qualities, like quantities, are determined by 'the feelings and judgments of the experienced' (X: 213; *U* 2: 8). And how do we know that a higher-quality pleasure (other things equal) is more valuable? As we should by now expect, Mill thinks the only criterion for this judgement, as with basic value judgements in general, is reflective practice – self-examination and discussion.

What often raises readers' hackles here is Mill's elitism: he thinks that only some people are competent to judge the quality, as against the quantity, of pleasure. But this elitism is the direct consequence of the developmental or progressive conception of human beings. One gains access to higher pleasures by cultivation of the feelings – so cultivation is required if one is to be a competent judge. Educating the feelings is neither merely indulging them, on the one hand, nor, on the other, disciplining them by a moral or religious standard external to them. It means working from within their spontaneity, criticising and strengthening them by their own internal standards. Those internal standards are also the standards by which quality of pleasure is judged. That there are such standards is just another application of Mill's epistemology of 'thinking from within'. (By the same token, objections to Mill's notion that there are such standards are often sceptical objections to the very idea of objective value.) All human beings, Mill thinks, can cultivate their feelings, but their affective sensibilities may point in different directions of development and give them different powers of enjoyment. If I, unlike you, get nothing out of poetry, there is a higher pleasure that is lost to me but accessible to you – but perhaps the reverse holds with respect to the higher pleasure of chess, or of athleticism.

There is no inconsistency in Mill's idea that he can reconcile hedonism and the liberal ideal, but that is not to say that hedonism is true. Also, an impression lingers that he in fact appeals to pluralistic intuitions. For example, he remarks that:

> [a] being of higher faculties requires more to make him happy, is capable probably of more acute suffering, and is certainly accessible to it at more points, than one of an inferior type; but in spite of these liabilities, he can never really wish to sink into what he feels to be a lower grade of existence.
>
> (X: 212; *U* 2: 6)

And he suggests that this preference can be explained by a sense of dignity that all human beings possess. It sounds then as though Mill thinks everyone has a desire for dignity, or self-respect, which is distinct from the desire for pleasure. In which case, by his own test, dignity is desirable as well as pleasure. Suppose that a being of higher faculties is faced with a choice: on the one hand, a life of considerable suffering, with no access to any of the higher pleasures which its faculties make it capable of appreciating, on the other, a cure which relieves its suffering but leaves it only with pleasures accessible by much simpler faculties (say, pleasant tunes and good food). Is Mill saying that in *all* such cases the life of suffering should be preferred? If he does adhere to hedonism, he should not say that. Cases must be possible in which life after the cure offers a stream of pleasures more valuable overall, taking quality as well as quantity into account, than the life of suffering in which one retains one's higher faculties but can *obtain* no higher pleasures. So if pleasure is all that matters, then in these cases one should choose the cure. Only if a separate desire for dignity trumps the desire for pleasure could such a choice be wrong.

2.5 Morality and justice

In response to Comte's rigoristic morality of service to others, we saw Mill distinguishing – with a good deal of emphasis – between what it is good and admirable, and what is morally obligatory (2.1). In Chapter 5 of *Utilitarianism*, he gives an analysis of moral obligation that makes room for this difference, and is interesting in its own right. He defines a moral wrong-doing as an act for which the individual ought to be punished 'if not by law, by the opinion of his fellow-creatures; if not by opinion, by the reproaches of his own conscience.' 'It is,' he continues, 'a part of the notion of Duty in every one of its forms, that a person may rightfully be compelled to fulfil it. Duty is a thing which may be *exacted* from a person, as one exacts a debt' (X: 246; *U* 5: 14).

Morality is concerned with that which an individual may be 'compelled', and not merely 'persuaded and exhorted', to do. The compulsion need not be legal compulsion – it can work through the attitudes of others or through one's own conscience. There are interesting differences between these three cases – criminality, blameability by others, and (appropriate) prohibition by one's own conscience – but Mill does not go into them. His basic idea is that a moral obligation of one kind or another exists in any case in which non-compliance ought to attract one or other of these sanctions. When ought it? According to Mill, when a sanction of one of these kinds promotes the general good.

He proceeds to define moral *rights* in terms of moral obligations. A person has a moral right to something if there is a moral obligation on society to protect them in their possession of that thing, or to guarantee it to them. And he defines *justice* in terms of rights: obligations of justice are distinguished from moral obligations in general by the existence of corresponding rights:

> Justice implies something which it is not only right to do, and wrong not to do, but which some individual person can claim from us as his moral right. ... Whenever there is a right, the case is one of justice.
>
> (X: 247; *U* 5: 15)

Upholding rights is one of society's vital tasks. For rights give us security – which is 'to every one's feelings the most vital of interests':

> This most indispensable of all necessaries, after physical nutriment, cannot be had, unless the machinery for providing it is kept unintermittedly in active play. Our notion,

35

therefore, of the claim we have on our fellow-creatures to join in making safe for us the very groundwork of our existence, gathers feelings around it so much more intense than those concerned in any of the more common cases of utility, that the difference in degree (as is often the case in psychology) becomes a real difference in kind.

(X: 251; *U* 5: 25)

Justice, Mill concludes: 'is a name for certain classes of moral rules, which concern the essentials of human well-being more nearly, and are therefore of more absolute obligation, than any other rules for the guidance of life' (X: 255; *U* 5: 32).

Mill spells out detailed and substantive views about what justice requires in many writings on various social questions. In *Utilitarianism*, he is concerned with the more abstract task of fitting morality, rights and justice into a utilitarian framework. His aim is to show how, consistently with that framework, justice-rights take priority over the direct pursuit of general utility by individuals or the state, just as they take priority over the private pursuit of personal ends. His position is thus more complex than that of philosophers in the Kantian tradition who assume, in John Rawls's phrase, that the right (or just) is prior to the good. For Mill, good is *philosophically* prior to right – but politically and socially, right constrains the pursuit of good.

This emphasis on the importance of security is exactly what one would expect from a liberal believer in the rule of law. There are, however, various difficulties in his analysis of the concepts. The strongest part of it is the characterisation of moral wrongness in terms of blameworthiness. That could and should be accepted by philosophers who are not utilitarians. But Mill wants to say more: that an action is blameworthy if and only if it promotes general well-being to blame it. This is to confuse the act of blame with the sentiment or attitude expressed in blame. Whether an action is morally wrong turns on whether that sentiment or attitude towards the agent is right. Whether it is prudent, expedient, etc. to blame the agent is another matter. The appropriateness of the action can be assessed by its consequences for general good. But the rightness of the sentiment cannot be. Similarly, you may be right to be angry with me but wrong to express that anger. What the utility principle governs is reasons for actions, not reasons for feelings.

Turning to justice and rights: Mill seems to me right to define justice in terms of rights in the way he does; in this regard he is only following many others. But his definition of right is unconvincing. It is not logically contradictory to say that society should guarantee Y to X even if X has no right to Y. The fact that X has a *right* to it is only one possible reason for guaranteeing it to him. Another possible reason is that he will blow up the world if we don't. More generally, there may be good reasons to guarantee something to people with a threat advantage, but that does not show they have a right to it.

Such examples are a special case of something that should not be too surprising: that attempts to reduce moral concepts to a theory of the good are unpersuasive. But does Mill actually need to try? He could take a weaker line. He could argue that the utilitarian theory of the good is the appropriate 'controller', in his word, of all our principles, ideals and ends. It is not their *generator*. They are not derived from it, or reducible to it, even though they are defeasible by it. They have relative autonomy. According to this utilitarian view, we have many normative principles governing action that are justified in their own terms, without derivation from the final good; but they must give way if they turn out to be systematically incompatible with that final good.

That is still a position that is utilitarian, at least in the sense that it would be rejected by strongly anti-utilitarian philosophers. And it makes sense to find the weakest version of utilitarianism that retains Mill's essential claims, with a view to making it the foundation for his liberalism. To that end we have given up hedonism, sum-total maximisation, and now the idea that morality should be derived from the good. But what really matters to Mill (arguably) is still retained: the primacy of the general good, impartially conceived, and a conception of that good in terms of what human beings do desire, in theory and practice. One might, furthermore, defend this position by applying Mill's own method of thinking from within. We have many aesthetic, ethical and moral dispositions that are neither reducible to others nor subversively explicable. There are many things we naturally find admirable, for example, as well as many things that we naturally find desirable, and then again types of action that we are naturally disposed to blame. By Mill's own method he should recognise the normative authority of all these dispositions.

3

Liberty

———•◆•———

3.1 *Liberty and popular sovereignty*

Of the classic texts of liberalism Mill's essay on *Liberty* stands in the first rank. It expounds a principle that has become, for many people, almost definitive of liberalism itself – I will call it the *Liberty Principle*. This principle says that individual freedom of conduct may be constrained by society only on specific grounds. They resist neat summary, as we shall see, but in broad terms they emerge as the following: the conduct in question is liable to harm others, or it involves a failure to act that can justly be considered a violation of duty to others, or it is a violation of the good manners required in a public place. All other grounds for interference are illegitimate.

Much of Mill's essay is an elucidation of what this means; the wide-ranging and penetrating way in which he does this is one reason for the essay's classic status. Another reason is Mill's account of the philosophical basis of the Liberty Principle. He justifies it in a highly distinctive way, arguing for it from the developmental view of human good considered in the previous chapter. The essay also contains a famous discussion of liberty of thought and discussion – this is done in a free-standing way which raises the interesting question of how liberty of discussion fits with the Liberty Principle. Does it simply fall under the Principle as a special case, covering one kind of action? Or is there something distinctive to be said about the activity of discussion, as Mill's separate treatment suggests?

On Liberty opens with a question that always preoccupied Mill, the question of liberty and democracy, of how we are to understand the doctrine of the sovereignty of the people. Mill's answer, his liberal critique of popular sovereignty, underlies everything else.

The struggle for liberty had historically been a struggle between subjects and Government. Liberty meant 'protection against the tyranny of political rulers'. Hence, to some radicals, limitations on the power of a *democratic* government seemed pointless. 'The nation did not need to be defended against its own will. There was no fear of its tyrannizing over itself' (XVIII: 217, 8; *L* 1: 2, 3). Mill thinks this a dangerous fallacy. The collective will is one thing, the will of an individual is another. If no limit to the authority of the former over the latter is recognised, there can be no principled check on popular authoritarianism.

This immediately pitches us into a fundamental conflict in modern politics: between liberal and collectivist theories of democracy. The liberal accepts that in the modern world, political authority must derive from the people, but holds that that popular sovereignty has principled limits. The collectivist doctrine is that popular sovereignty has no such limits – 'all power to the people'. The conflict between these two doctrines first came into clear view in the French Revolution. The Liberty Principle expresses the doctrine of its liberal wing, and is in fact stated in the French Assembly's Declaration of Rights of 1789:

> Political Liberty consists in the power of doing whatever does not injure another. Thus the exercise of the natural rights of every man has no other limits than those which

are necessary to secure to every other member of society enjoyment of the same rights.

Mill did not present his doctrine as new, and anticipated that to some people 'it may have the air of a truism' (XVIII: 226; L 1: 14). But like other liberals of the time, especially liberals in France who had the excesses of Jacobinism in the French Revolution, and of Bonapartism after it, fresh in their minds, he wanted to reaffirm the doctrine and have it specifically acknowledged in democratic states.

For democracy threatens a new form of tyranny: a 'tyranny of the majority' (the phrase is de Tocqueville's). Such tyranny might express itself in majoritarian political despotism. But it might also be more insidiously practised as a social tyranny, which leaving 'fewer means of escape, penetrating much more deeply into the details of life, and enslaving the soul itself' could be 'more formidable than many kinds of political oppression' (XVIII: 220; L 1: 5). Given Mill's definition of moral obligation (2.5), this means that limits must be recognised on morality as well as law. The fundamental question is how to define those limits. Many 'progressive thinkers' tend to shrug off the question; they are more concerned with deciding what society *should* like or dislike, than with 'questioning whether its likings or dislikings should be a law to individuals' (XVIII: 222; L 1: 7). As far as Mill is concerned, they make a profound mistake.

3.2 *The Liberty Principle*

Mill fires off with a powerful statement:

> The object of this Essay is to assert one very simple principle, as entitled to govern absolutely the dealings of society with the individual in the way of compulsion and

control, whether the means used be physical force in the form of legal penalties, or the moral coercion of public opinion. That principle is, that the sole end for which mankind are warranted, individually or collectively, in interfering with the liberty of action of any of their number, is self-protection. That the only purpose for which power can be rightfully exercised over any member of a civilised community, against his will, is to prevent harm to others. His own good, either physical or moral, is not a sufficient warrant. He cannot rightfully be compelled to do or forbear because it will be better for him to do so, because it will make him happier, because, in the opinion of others, to do so would be wise, or even right. These are good reasons for remonstrating with him, or reasoning with him, or persuading him, or entreating him, but not for compelling him, or visiting him with any evil in case he do otherwise. To justify that, the conduct from which it is desired to deter him must be calculated to produce evil to someone else. The only part of the conduct of any one, for which he is amenable to society, is that which concerns others. In the part which merely concerns himself, his independence is, of right, absolute. Over himself, over his own body and mind, the individual is sovereign.

(XVIII: 223–4; *L* 1: 9)

He immediately limits the domain of the principle – it does not apply to children or to 'backward states of society'.

Despotism is a legitimate mode of government in dealing with barbarians, provided the end be their improvement, and the means justified by actually effecting that end. Liberty, as a principle, has no application to any state of things

42

anterior to the time when mankind have become capable of
being improved by free and equal discussion.

(XVIII: 224; *L* 1: 10)

This remark is not a piece of unthinking prejudice. It reflects
Mill's historical conception of progress towards freedom. He
thinks of it as a process of mental and moral development, which
takes place within individuals but also at the level of social norms.
Liberty can prevail in a society only when 'barbarian' self-assertion and its oppressive and violent social structures have been
overcome. Prior to that, the best a nation can hope for is the
despotic good offices of 'an Akhbar or a Charlemagne'. Histori-
cism in this sense was a deeply considered part of Mill's thinking;
we shall come back to it in the next chapter.

The statement of the Liberty Principle itself is so ringing that it
is tempting to treat it as though all elucidation and development
in the rest of the essay was redundant. That would be wrong.
Mill produces no final and canonical statement of his principle.
He relies on ordinary words in their ordinary meaning, adding
further explanations or qualifications as becomes necessary, and
closing the essay with examples of how to apply the principle in
practice. It all still leaves much room for interpretation, as is
always the case with a basic political idea. We can pick out three
themes.

First, the most prominent and celebrated theme is rejection of
'paternalist' reasons for compulsion, that is, reasons directed at the
individual's own good. For example, banning drug use on the
grounds that it is harmful to the user is forbidden by the Liberty
Principle. Furthermore, Mill intends the Principle to apply to all
joint activities between freely consenting adults: so it also strikes
down any interference based on the claim that the participating
individuals who consent are harming each other. It does not of
course strike down intervention based on an action's harmful

effects on third parties who are *not* freely participating – but nor does it follow that all such interventions are justified. Their justification will depend on the balance of advantages. And Mill is well aware that something that is in fact disapproved of for other reasons may be persecuted under the claim that it is harmful to others. The effect of the Liberty Principle is to place the onus of proof on those who make that claim. Take suicide (not one of Mill's own examples). Plainly, it may be wrong to commit suicide if others will suffer as a result. But if we accept the Liberty Principle that does not justify a legal or moral prohibition of suicide itself, irrespective of such effects. Nor, by the consenting adults principle, does it justify prohibition of assisted suicide. If the real objection is not the effect on others, but rather that our lives do not belong to us to dispose of but to God, then we are back to the fundamental issue of ultimate sovereignty over one's own life. Mill gives it to the individual, some communitarians give it to society, some religious believers to God.

The Liberty Principle also rejects interventions on grounds of offence to other people's feelings. A prohibition on the eating of pork in a Muslim society, or on forms of worship other than Catholic in a Roman Catholic society (two of Mill's many examples, XVIII: 283; *L* 4:12ff), if put forward on grounds of their offensiveness to the majority, would infringe the Liberty Principle. But – and here is the second theme we should notice – Mill accepts that it can be right to prohibit public behaviour merely on grounds of its intrusiveness, rather than its harmfulness. He thinks that acts which

> are a violation of good manners ... coming thus within the category of offences against others, may rightly be prohibited. Of this kind are offences against decency; on which it is unnecessary to dwell, the rather as they are only connected indirectly with our subject, the objection to

publicity being equally strong in the case of many actions
not in themselves condemnable, nor supposed to be so.

(XVIII: 295–6; *L* 5: 7)

This prim remark arrives rather clumsily, as one of a series of
qualifications in the final chapter that are intended to clarify various
issues about the Principle's application. It has considerably more
importance than that suggests. Moreover, Mill's choice of the
phrase 'offences against others' has caused needless confusion. The
point about them is not that they harm others (in the way that
smoking has secondary effects on others' health, for example), or
even, exactly, that they are offensive. It is simply that they are *intrusions*
on other individuals in a public or shared space, and thus a 'violation
of good manners', since good manners in public places are in part
about not intruding in an unwelcome manner on others' attention.

What this then calls for is a more general account of the notion
of intrusiveness, imposition, or nuisance. It will have a lot to do
with local expectations, but those expectations themselves have
to be justifiable. If a railway carriage is designated as a quiet place,
we are not violating the liberty right of an individual who insists
on having loud mobile phone conversations when we eject him
from it. That is so, even though he neither *harms* nor necessarily
offends anyone by his conversation. But the legitimacy of stopping
him does not arise simply from the existence of prior agreement
or warning. Quiet carriages do not infringe the rights of noisy
people, whereas 'Whites only' carriages do infringe the rights of
non-white people. It is not enough to say that non-whites have
been warned. Noise can be properly counted a nuisance or intrusion, whereas the presence of a non-white person in a carriage
cannot be, however offended whites may feel. Intrusion, in other
words, is a normative concept.

Mill spends no time on these important issues. Still, the principles whereby he distinguishes between *illegitimate* prohibition of

private or public behaviour simply on the grounds that it offends people, and *legitimate* prohibition of nuisance behaviour in a public place, are intuitive and not that controversial. There would, for example, be a fairly wide consensus among broadly liberal-minded people that a play or a novel that is offensive to the feelings of some religious groups cannot be banned solely on that ground, and that the state has an obligation to prevent or punish attacks on the author. Those who do not wish to see the play or read the novel do not have to do so. It is not an intrusion or nuisance in a common space.

In contrast, when Mill sides with liberty against paternalist intervention he takes a line in favour of liberty that is stronger than much current opinion. A couple of examples will help to make that clear. The requirement that motor cyclists wear helmets pretty clearly violates the Liberty Principle. It won't do to reply that those injuries to a motor cyclist that arise from his not wearing a helmet impose on collectively provided health care, and that this 'harms' us all by raising the cost of that provision. In the first place that dangerously stretches the notion of 'harm'. We made a democratic decision to provide collective cover: the costs we incur as a result are down to us. Second, the legislation does not exempt people who are prepared to eliminate extra costs to others by taking out private insurance, or simply by waiving their right to be treated in case of accident. A common argument for compulsion runs as follows: if a person without a helmet does suffer a resulting injury we will have an obligation to provide the care, *even if* he has waived his right to it. That being so, we can insist that he takes precautions. This may be a good argument, but it departs from Mill's Liberty Principle. He allows for no such line of thought.

Next, take drug use. Here a case for legal prohibition or control can be made on grounds of likely harm to others. But often the case is made on the simple grounds that taking drugs is bad for the drug-taker. Sometimes, more interestingly, it is made on the basis that drug-addiction is a form of self-enslavement which itself reduces personal freedom. The latter argument should have force for a liberal; it is similar to that of 'new liberals' in Britain at the end of the nineteenth century. They wanted to introduce temperance laws controlling the consumption of alcohol precisely, as they argued, to protect 'positive freedom'. They were quite consciously diverging from Mill. His position in *On Liberty* is that drunkenness as such is not 'a fit subject for legislative interference' (XVIII: 295: *L* 5: 6) – though he thinks that a person found guilty of drink-induced violence can subsequently be fined for getting drunk again, and that crimes of violence induced by drink may be punished more severely. A similar approach to drugs would legalise drug use, license drug sales, but introduce relatively more severe penalties for drug-induced offences. And a public health campaign against drug-taking would not violate the Liberty Principle, given Mill's view, which we'll shortly discuss, that we have an obligation to educate each other about what is good.

The third, and very important, aspect of the Liberty Principle is its anti-rigorist side. We saw how firmly Mill distinguishes between actions that can be regarded as moral obligations, and actions that are praiseworthy but not obligatory (2.1). That distinction is vital for the Liberty Principle.

The Liberty Principle requires Mill to distinguish between actions that concern only the individual and actions that concern others. Some critics object that no such distinction can be made. This objection, however, is too brusque to be convincing. Obviously the distinction is discussable at the edges, but many of the most important distinctions are discussable at the edges. We make this one all the time, for example, when we distinguish between what is your business and what isn't. Clearly, though, the distinction must in turn rely on a common-sense distinction between harming others and omitting to benefit them. If harming or causing evil to others and refraining from benefiting them were morally equivalent, the Liberty Principle would lose all force. A failure to benefit others could always be construed as a 'harm' to others, and hence the state, or coercive public opinion, could not be stopped by the Liberty Principle from compelling people to do anything that is beneficial to others and from penalising them if they did not. There would be no such thing as a domain of actions that concern only the individual himself. That is just the sort of liberticide that Mill feared from Comte.

So the Liberty Principle firmly rests on this basic distinction between harming and omitting to benefit. At the same time, however, we certainly think that there are things that people have a positive obligation to do for the benefit of other individuals, or in general for the public good, and we don't want the Liberty Principle to strike down such obligations just because, when someone fails to do these things, he isn't actually harming others in any ordinary sense of harm. Mill recognises this, and puts down some general principles – rather more carefully than in the case of public nuisance but still without developing what a present-day political theorist might call a *theory* of the obligations of citizenship. So, for example, he says that everyone may be required to bear their fair share 'of the labours and sacrifices incurred for defending the society or its members from injury or molestation' (XVIII: 276; L 4: 3).

Such obligations may be required by law, and would be recognised by libertarians who endorse very minimalist notions of the role of the state and law. But Mill goes further. In the first place, he is quite willing to envisage legally enforceable taxation for purely redistributive purposes, in a way that the libertarian wing of liberalism disallows. This issue is not central to *On Liberty*, but is clear in his writings on distributive justice, which we will come to in the next chapter.

Another important point is the following. It would be, Mill says, 'a great misunderstanding' of his doctrine

> to suppose that it is one of selfish indifference, which pre-
> tends that human beings have no business with each other's
> conduct in life, and that they should not concern them-
> selves about the well-doing or well-being of one another,
> unless their own interest is involved ... Human beings owe
> to each other help to distinguish the better from the worse,
> and encouragement to choose the former rather than the
> latter.

He means the better or worse for oneself. There are 'self-regarding virtues', qualities required for full self-development, as well as 'social' ones, and 'It is equally the business of education to cultivate both' (XVIII: 276–7; *L* 4: 4).

So we have a moral obligation to help in educating each other how best to live. Mill takes that duty very seriously, to the point where some have seen his eagerness as incipiently authoritarian. That is a mistake, for while Mill's idea of how far we should lec-ture each other about self-regarding virtues and vices may be alarmingly robust, he has a relevant distinction in place. Morality is concerned with that which an individual may be 'compelled', and not merely 'persuaded and exhorted', to do (2.5). (This dis-tinction, certainly, is another one that is importantly discussable at the edges, but again that does not mean it can do no work.) The apparently paradoxical, but actually consistent, outcome is that we have no moral obligation to cultivate the self-regarding virtues in ourselves, but do have a moral obligation to help each other to cultivate them. Society may censure us if we fail in that duty; it may also, compatibly with the Liberty Principle, raise taxes to ensure that an education in the self-regarding virtues is made available by the state. Whether it should do so is a question of efficient policy, not a question touching on liberty. So Mill is not an ethical neutralist about the state (5.4). But what the Liberty Principle certainly does rule out is any intervention which *prevents* a group of citizens from justly advancing their own ethical and cultural ideals – however harmful to themselves these may actually be.

Finally, we should sample the way in which Mill seeks to explicate his Liberty Principle over a wide range of applications. In its absence, he thinks, 'liberty is often granted where it should be withheld, as well as withheld where it should be granted' (XVIII: 301; *L* 5: 12):

> When we compare the strange respect of mankind for liberty, with their strange want of respect for it, we might imagine that a man had an indispensable right to do harm to others, and no right at all to please himself without giving pain to anyone.
>
> (XVIII: 304–5; *L* 5: 15)

One of his case studies is family relations. As we would expect from Mill's lifelong battle for the rights of women, he has in mind the 'almost despotic power of husbands over wives' (XVIII: 301; *L* 5: 12). The remedy is exactly equal rights for both. Less comfortably for current opinion, however, he thinks that having and rearing children incurs important obligations whose enforcement should not checked by 'misplaced notions of liberty' (XVIII: 304; *L* 5: 15). Prohibiting marriage to those who cannot show they have the means to support children would not, he says, exceed the legitimate powers of the state. Nowadays in Western societies marriage and procreation have come apart, so that would be a rather bizarre policy. But Mill might very well have favoured the more recent suggestion that a state licence should be required for those wishing to have children.

Education continues the theme. The whole discussion is an important illustration of Mill's attitudes. Society has a duty to enforce universal education, but it is not the state that should provide it. 'That the whole or any large part of the education of the people should be in state hands, I go as far as anyone in deprecating' (XVIII: 302; *L* 5: 13). What the state should provide is financial support for children's education, in part or where necessary in whole – and 'public examinations, extending to all children, and beginning at an early age' (XVIII: 303; *L* 5: 14). If children are unable to read by a fixed age, parents should be fined unless they have some excuse. Later examinations could range over a variety of subjects but should test understanding and factual knowledge, not doctrinal orthodoxy. It is the danger of excessive state power in forming minds and thereby exerting mental despotism that dominates this part of Mill's discussion: 'A general State education is a mere contrivance for moulding people to be exactly like one another' (XVIII: 302; *L* 5: 13). State-run schools should exist, if at all, only as competing experiments among others and to set standards of excellence for the private sector.

In general, Mill's position is that intervention, even when not inconsistent with the Liberty Principle, should be avoided where possible: because things are mostly better done by individuals, because when they are done by individuals that is itself an education in self-governance, and because adding to state power is usually an evil. However, that still leaves him with a range of cases where he thinks, against free marketeers of the time, that legislative intervention can be appropriate. An example is legislation to restrict the working week. Here the point is that such agreed restriction may be in everyone's interests but will be unstable if voluntary. Needless to say, however, legislation that requires respect for the Sabbath, or limits what leisure activities can be done on that day, is something Mill opposes.

3.3 *Spontaneity, conflict, progress*

In his *Autobiography*, Mill described *On Liberty* as:

> a kind of philosophic textbook of a single truth, which the
> changes progressively taking place in modern society bring
> out into ever stronger relief: the importance, to man and
> society, of a large variety in types of character, and of
> giving full freedom to human nature to expand itself in
> innumerable and conflicting directions.

(1: 259)

Given the range of applications we have just been surveying, it
turns out that exposition of a single truth can be complicated and
unexpected! But the third chapter of *On Liberty*, 'Of individuality,
as one of the elements of well-being', does indeed focus on the
single philosophic truth.

Mill, we saw, insists that the case for the Liberty Principle
derives from an account of human well-being (2.3). But our
understanding of well-being must take full account of human
beings' developmental or 'progressive' nature. The argument is
two-fold. First, there is the Millian principle: that the fullest
development of potential opens the way to the highest forms of
well-being. Then there is the liberal ideal of what constitutes
fullest personal development. Its distinctive feature is its stress on
wholeness – laying as much stress on the education of feeling as
on the education of reason and will (2.3).

Whereas thinking and willing, as they develop, tend to con-
verge on universal principles, feelings, and thus personal ends,
preferences and ideals, diverge. Since the emotional potentialities
of different human beings differ, cultivation proliferates indi-
vidualities and forms of experience. Education of the feelings is an
element in the fullest self-development and produces diversity; so,

by the Millian principle, diversity is an element of the highest well-being:

> different persons ... require different conditions for their spiritual development; and can no more exist healthily in the same moral, than all the variety of plants can in the same physical, atmosphere and climate. The same things which are helps to one person towards the cultivation of his higher nature, are hindrances to another. The same mode of life is a healthy excitement to one, keeping all his faculties of action and enjoyment in their best order, while to another it is a distracting burthen, which suspends or crushes all internal life. Such are the differences among human beings in their sources of pleasure, their suscept- ibilities of pain, and the operation on them of different physical and moral agencies, that unless there is a corre- sponding diversity in their modes of life, they neither obtain their fair share of happiness, nor grow up to the mental, moral, and aesthetic stature of which their nature is capable.
>
> (XVIII: 270; *L* 3: 14)

In face of this diversity of self-realising paths, people must judge their best path for themselves. That does not mean that they should judge in isolation. One would not expect Mill, given his philosophical view of free inquiry, to dismiss the lessons of custom, discussion, and the experience of others. In particular, a society with a wide variety of characters and 'experiments of living' thereby has an empirical test of the worth for well-being of many different modes of life – a rich database of lessons.

Mill is splendidly individualistic and elitist about culture. All creativity comes from individuals, and from a few individuals only. Neither custom nor any kind of bureaucratic cultural institution can substitute for the gifted few: 'But these few are the salt of the earth; without them human life would become a stagnant pool.' Genius, however, 'can only breathe freely in an *atmosphere* of freedom' (XVIII: 267; L 3: 11). The vital question for modern democracies is whether they can preserve the highest forms of creativity:

> No government by a democracy or a numerous aristocracy, either in its political acts or in the opinions, qualities, and tone of mind which it fosters, ever did or could rise above mediocrity, except in so far as the sovereign many have let themselves be guided (which in their best times they always have done) by the counsels and influence of a more highly gifted and instructed One or Few. The initiation of all wise and noble things must come from individuals; generally at first from some one individual. The honour and glory of the average man is ... that he can respond internally to wise and noble things, and be led to them with his eyes open.
>
> (XVIII: 269; L 3: 13)

It is not Mill's point that the gifted 'One or Few' should have power to force their initiatives on others. The point is precisely the contrary one – in safeguarding the freedom of each individual to draw up his own plan of life, society also safeguards the gifted few and their experiments of living; it gives them 'freedom to point out the way', but not the 'power of compelling others into it' (XVIII: 269; L 3: 13).

It is good, too, that they should point out a variety of ways. Progress is not achieved by a united avant-garde phalanx of the creative, marching down a single road. Mill strongly favoured the conflict theory of progress (as one might call it), a theory that French liberal historians had developed, as an explanation of

European progressiveness in comparison with the stagnation of other ancient civilisations:

> What has made the European family of nations an improv-ing, instead of a stationary portion of mankind? Not any superior excellence in them, which, when it exists, exists as the effect, not as the cause; but their remarkable diversity of character and culture ... Europe is, in my judgement, wholly indebted to this plurality of paths for its progressive and many-sided development.
>
> (XVIII: 274; *L* 3: 18)

Mill's *liberal elitism* is the diametric opposite of authoritarian popu-lism. He combines it with a civic and political egalitarianism which we shall examine in the next chapter. Liberal elitism recognises the objectivity and hierarchy of values, the vital dis-tances between great, good and bad, the insight and creativity of the few. It wants intellectual and moral authority to be widely recognised but gives it no coercive social or political power. Mill feared the authoritarian and populist tendencies of democracy. But he believed – with level-headed calmness, or with compla-cency, depending on one's point of view – that if his principles of liberty were rigorously upheld, there would be enough openness and freedom for intellectual and moral insight to establish its natural authority. The Liberty Principle, together with liberty of discussion, would safeguard the conditions for spiritual and moral progress, liberating originality and genius and encouraging plenty of healthy conflict, disagreement, and dissent.

Here, then, are some Millian propositions:

1 The greatest fullness of life comes through developing one's nature – in all aspects of feeling, reason and will.
2 Aesthetic, intellectual and moral self-development is open to all.

3 Open and universal culture requires unchecked diversity and dissent.
4 It requires contributions of the highest order of greatness. These can only be made by a creative few, and are most favoured in an atmosphere of freedom.
5 Democracy without an entrenched Liberty Principle threatens mediocre conformism, and even a political despotism of the majority.

3.4 *Liberty of thought and discussion*

There is a puzzle about how the second chapter of *On Liberty*, which deals with liberty of thought and discussion, fits in – not just about how Mill thinks it fits in but about how it *should* fit in. Is liberty of discussion just a special case of the general Liberty Principle? Or is it a supplementary principle, which gives a greater degree of protection to communication and discussion than other actions receive from the Liberty Principle? And if so, why? What is so special about communicative as against any other kind of action? Once we have spelt out a general principle of liberty of action, why do we need a special principle of liberty of discussion?

Mill says that liberty of discussion is a 'single branch' of his 'general thesis' (XVIII: 227; *L* 1:16). But in practice, he seems to think that liberty of discussion merits stronger safeguards than liberty of action in general, and he argues for it on separate grounds. Any restriction on free discussion impedes the progress of truth and impoverishes the qualities of mind of those whose access to discussion is restricted. Even where it does not positively sustain error and block truth's growth, it still draws the life from it, or distorts it by stopping it from flourishing unrestrictedly on all its sides.

Why do these considerations protect discussion in particular over action in general? The main point, it seems, concerns the social importance of *dialogue*. Dialogue, unconstrained truth-seeking discussion, is nothing but the social expression of free thought. Given human fallibility, and the distortions and manipulations to which free thought is subject, only continued full exposure to free discussion can give us continued rational warrant for our beliefs. Socially possessed truth and disinterested, rational qualities of mind among citizens are public goods. Hence, protection of free dialogue is based directly on its social benefit, rather than indirectly, by an argument going through the rights of the individual.

These are very good thoughts and Mill puts them very memorably. But there are great difficulties in formulating an acceptable principle. How should we take into account various issues about incitement, intimidation, confidentiality, defamation, privacy, trustworthiness in testimony, and so on? On this question, of formulation, Mill does not say much to help us; sadly he does not provide the detailed discussion of the applications and limits of liberty of discussion that he gives for the Liberty Principle itself. He does say this:

> No one pretends that actions should be as free as opinions. On the contrary, even opinions lose their immunity when the circumstances in which they are expressed are such as to constitute their expressions a positive instigation to some mischievous act. An opinion that corn dealers are starvers of the poor, or that private property is robbery, ought to be unmolested when simply circulated through the press, but may justly incur punishment when delivered orally to an excited mob assembled before the house of a corn-dealer, or when handed about among the same mob in the form of a placard.
>
> (XVIII: 260; L 3: 1)

This has two points of interest. It suggests that Mill does think expression of opinion should be more protected than action in general, and it gives some indication of when it can nonetheless be penalised. Note that the interesting phrase 'positive instigation to some mischievous act', when taken with his example of the excited mob, has two disparate elements: (1) the notion of incitement; and (2) the point that the audience is not in a rational state. Mill links the two; the mob before the corn-dealer's house is not in a rational state and that (by implication) is why, in those circumstances, the opinion constitutes a 'positive instigation to a mischievous act'. But they can be uncoupled. Suppose that an invited speaker at the philosophy seminar argues that political assassination is not always wrong. Beginning with the usual examples, such as Hitler, Stalin, etc., he warms to his theme and eloquently puts the case that the Prime Minister or the President is causing so much harm to so many people that anyone who bumps him off – and here he glances around meaningfully – would be a public benefactor. Is this a 'positive instigation to a mischievous act'? That is literally what it is. Is it all right to prohibit the expression of such opinions by law, in all circumstances including philosophy seminars? No. And bearing in mind that Mill is interested in the legitimacy of moral as well as legal sanction, what should we say on that score? Should we say that this speaker was doing something morally wrong simply in propounding this opinion to the seminar? Again I think not. We might think him wild and dangerous, we might think of warning him, or others about him. Depending on how we read his intentions, we might disapprove of him. But we should not try to prevent him from speaking. He does, after all, make us think harder about when political assassination is legitimate, and that is the kind of thing (among many others) that philosophy seminars should do.

One line of thought, suggested by this kind of example, says that the key question in such cases is not, was there reason to think harm would occur?, but, was there reason to think the audience was in a rational state? Was it able to assess what it heard, and decide for itself how to act? If so, its actions are its own responsibility and no-one else's. In contrast, the 'excited mob' is not fully responsible for its actions, and in those circumstances we fall back on the Liberty Principle. (Which, of course, still provides a lot of protection – it forbids, for example, restricting speech merely because it is found offensive, or merely because it incites 'religious hatred' as against actual violence.)

Something is right about this, but it is plainly too simple. If a person I know to be intent on blowing up his neighbours asks me how to manufacture a cost-effective bomb, it is no restriction on free speech to require that I do not give him the information – and that applies even if I'm speaking to a highly rational murderer, fully in control of himself. Information should not be made available to people who will foreseeably use it to carry out an existing intention to commit a wrongful act. My responsibility arises because I should have regarded the situation as one in which I am giving someone a means to carry out a pre-intended wrong-doing, not as one in which I am entering into a discussion, for example, with bomb-disposal experts. Formulating a principle of liberty of discussion should take account of that distinction – and of many others that are equally hard to formulate. Take the right to privacy. Whether or not we think it should be illegal, it is surely morally objectionable to broadcast information about an individual's private life which he or she would prefer to remain private, unless an important public interest is served in doing so. So a notion of public interest comes into play, which the political philosopher could usefully try to clarify – it is, for example, not the same as what interests the public. And given the skill Mill shows in illustrating the applications of the Liberty Principle, it would have been very interesting to have from him a similarly considered discussion of Liberty of Discussion. He does not do that, nor has it ever been very successfully done. Perhaps this is not a subject on which we can get a worked-out principle, as against a list of considerations that need to be kept in balance. That does not make it a less important question for political philosophy to address.

But let's go back to what Mill does do. Allowing that free discussion has the good effects Mill notes, what if it simultaneously fosters the dissemination of harmful error – of crazy beliefs about harmful diets or drugs, enslaving religious cults, paranoid suspicions about the motives of unpopular minorities, or irrational nationalistic obsessions? Can there not, moreover, be harmful truths? Even if it were granted that in a world of perfectly reasonable people, the truth would never be harmful, we know that we do not live in such a world.

There is a tension between unrestricted liberty of discussion and intellectual and moral authority. It is a question of how that authority can achieve a healthy influence. Can it do so in unrestricted open dialogue, or does it need to be instituted in a church, university, ministry or party academy? In Mill's vision, intellectual or moral authority commands freely given respect and spontaneous assent, by citizens who may lack relevant competence or knowledge, but can recognise it when they see it. A common objection to this ideal of democratic intellect (perhaps nowadays more often felt than formulated) is that it assumes unrealistically high standards of integrity and disinterested rationality from too many people on too many subjects. The more struck we are by human irrationality and ignorance – and by its unequal distribution – the more inclined we shall be to restrict open dialogue on this or that important subject to an appropriate elite – at least initially, while the main principles are being worked out.

Yet any elite is itself a group of fallible and corruptible human beings. It will develop the interests and solidarity of a social class, and uncriticisable ideological doctrines to sustain those interests. Dialogue appeals to the common reason of *all* human beings; to leave it in the hands of one group is to provide no mechanism for eliminating the particular distorting perspectives of that group. Further, rationality and responsibility are qualities developed by education and practice. People who are shut out of free discussion are stunted and diminished – they are prone to the diseases of reason, to paranoia, to the defensive aggression that arises from ignorance and low self-esteem, to exploitation by demagogues.

Mill was absolutely not a thinker to whom the dangers of unrestricted open dialogue had never occurred. Society, he thinks, needs beliefs and feelings which provide enduring rallying points of allegiance and inspiration. Can such sources of allegiance survive if there is total liberty to criticise all sources of allegiance? That is the danger of disintegration; but there is also the danger of uncritical integration. In a democracy, does unrestricted open dialogue check mediocre conformism, or does it, on the contrary, accelerate democracy's tendency to sell out to celebrity, the politics of simple-minded causes, the glamour of simplistic myths? Or rather, since both occur, which prevails?

Mill thought hard about these crucial questions, throughout his adult life. They were central to his assessment of modernity (4.4, 5.3). That should be remembered when we consider that his most extended discussion of the matter comes down so unambiguously for liberty of discussion.

3.5 *Personal independence*

A utilitarian of more authoritarian bent than Mill might well hold that the Liberty Principle is positively incompatible with the Greatest Happiness Principle – in particular, that an element of well-judged paternalism often advances the general happiness. True, Mill cannily restricts the Liberty Principle to societies in which people are 'capable of being improved by free and equal discussion'. But, one might reply, what if they are then still capable of being improved in other ways too?

Some liberals may say that this question cannot be safely left to utilitarians to debate. For these liberals, the foundation of liberty is not utility but natural right. They must face the philosophical utilitarian's argument (2.5) that all principles are defeasible by the general good, and that rights themselves flourish only if they defend essential human interests.

Among these interests, however, we should factor in personal independence, our demand for a sphere in which what we say goes. It is expressed in the response, 'Who are you to tell me what to do, if it does no harm or injury to other people?' This demand for personal independence is liable to take unkindly even to well-meant and well-merited advice. It certainly draws the line at forcible paternalist intervention.

Personal independence is not a pre-moral notion; it distinguishes between sovereignty over my own life and sovereignty over anyone else's. Suppose I want to go for a walk and I want you to come with me. To stop me from going because it's bad for me would infringe my independence. But it is not infringed if you refuse to go – even though I don't get everything I want. Whether I go for a walk is up to me, whether you accompany me is up to you. I would step over implicitly understood limits if I tried too pressingly to get you to go. In our personal relations we make and understand such distinctions all the time. Where the private spheres of different individuals overlap, they cease to be private, and become a part of public or common space, thereby implying that each independent individual has a say in the use of that space. This explains the difference between what it is permissible for me to do in a public park, on a train, and in my house. In a public space some acts can be prohibited because they invasively privatise, take over, that space.

It is the desirability of personal independence that makes plausible the natural rights model of liberty. But Mill can say, as ever, that personal independence is desirable because desired. It is an element of distinctively human well-being, not an abstractly intuited political right:

> He who would rightly appreciate the worth of personal independence as an element of happiness should consider the value he himself puts on it as an ingredient of his own. There is no subject on which there is a greater habitual difference of judgement between a man judging for himself, and the same man judging for other people. When he hears others complaining that they are not allowed freedom of action – that their own will has not sufficient influence in the regulation of their affairs – his inclination is, to ask, what are their grievances? what positive damage they sustain? and in what respect they consider their affairs to be mismanaged? and if they fail to make out, in answer to these questions, what appears to him a sufficient case, he turns a deaf ear, and regards their complaint as the fanciful querulousness of people whom nothing reasonable will satisfy. But he has quite a different standard of judgement when he is deciding for himself.
>
> (XXI: 336–7)

Is personal independence valuable to us only as an element of happiness, though? That is an issue between Mill's hedonism and the pluralist view of well-being. If Mill is right, a reduction of my personal independence harms me only if it makes me less happy overall. If the pluralist is right, and personal independence is something I reasonably desire separately from my desire for happiness, then it may be best for me, in some cases, to trade off some happiness to maintain my personal independence.

Either way, personal independence is not an abstract right but a part of 'utility in the largest sense'. The Liberty Principle does not follow from it as a direct corollary, because in principle the benefit of a paternalistic intervention could outweigh the cost to personal independence. But Mill can certainly argue that personal independence is so essential to human well-being, both in itself and for its good consequences, that it should be respected as a right. Which, of course, is what he does. Personal independence, moral freedom and individual spontaneity are the values that underpin *On Liberty*.

4

Modernity

————•◆•————

4.1 Interpreting the modern world

At the beginning of the nineteenth century ethical thought became engrossed in history. Unsurprisingly, given the great events of 1775–1825: the emergence of constitutional democracy in America, the French Revolution, the rise and fall of Napoleon, Europe's revolutionary wars, and the various European attempts at liberal constitutions. That this was a time of crisis and transition to a new age was a truism of the time itself. But what would be the shape of the emerging modern world? To what hopes or anxieties did it give rise? And what was to be done?

In France and especially Germany, philosophy itself became, for a time, historical. Process, narrative, becoming, appeared not just as fundamentals of human life but as metaphysical categories. Nietzsche later spoke for pretty much the whole century when he said, 'What separates us from Kant, as from Plato and Leibniz, is that we believe only in Becoming – in intellectual matters too; we are historical through and through'. This new historical consciousness went with a depth of self-consciousness, a new sense of the problematic nature of 'self' itself, of the historicity and mutability of human beings. It transformed Mill's thinking but it did not remove his adherence to Enlightenment fundamentals. He says in his *Autobiography* that he never joined in the reaction against the eighteenth century, 'but kept as firm a hold of one side of the truth as I took of the other. ... Goethe's device, "many-sidedness," was one which I would most willingly, at this period, have taken for mine' (1: 171). He was right about the firmness with which he grasped both sides: the ability to see many countervailing issues in proportion is one of his great strengths as political philosopher. No-one has it perfectly, especially on questions as great as this. Nevertheless, Mill's examination of Enlightenment and counter-Enlightenment was deep, and the effect of the latter on him sustained and profound.

He discusses them in a pair of essays on Bentham and Coleridge: Bentham, the great figure of the radical Enlightenment, Coleridge, the eloquent spokesman of the counter-Enlightenment. His estimate of Bentham voices the nineteenth century's sense of its own greater maturity. He heaps praise on Bentham's analytic and critical powers, but he thinks him 'a boy to the last':

> [Self-consciousness] that daemon of the men of genius of our time, from Wordsworth to Byron, from Goethe to Chateaubriand, and to which this age owes so much both of its cheerful and its mournful wisdom, never was awakened in him. How much of human nature slumbered in him he knew not, neither can we know. He had never been made alive to the unseen influences which were acting on himself, nor consequently on his fellow-creatures. Other ages and other nations were a blank to him for purposes of instruction. He measured them but by one standard; their knowledge of facts, and their capability to take correct views of utility, and merge all other objects in it.
>
> (X: 92)

Thus wrote Mill in his early thirties. He would later have been less cutting, but he could not have returned to Bentham's mental world even if he had wanted to. Mill's questions about history, humanity and human good were nineteenth-century, late-modern questions, shaped by the experience of revolution and Romanticism.

How did the new self-consciousness address its new questions? There were broadly 'communitarian' and 'liberal' responses, and there was an increasingly sharp divergence, on the communitarian side, between 'right' and 'left'. We must not make too much of such labels of course – nor were these the only responses – nonetheless, these particular differences of outlook have proved seminal and still shape our thinking.

Right communitarians took it that the French Revolution's descent into terror and despotism flowed from deep flaws in the Enlightenment's ethical vision: its unhistorical individualism and rationalism, and the shallow and limited notion of freedom to which this gave rise. In this regard, the two most influential thinkers were Comte in France and Hegel in Germany. They shared a conception of human societies as historically developing organic wholes, and an anti-individualist social metaphysics. Neither wanted a return to the *ancien régime* or even thought it possible (there were sections of conservative opinion that did want it, but the right communitarianism we are considering differs from these). Both thought that the advent of modernity was philosophically inevitable; that it must affect every aspect of social and mental life, and that it was to be welcomed as progressive in its effect on the development of human beings. Yet revolutionary terror had starkly highlighted the potential for collapse in modernising societies. The crucial new questions were how to reconcile the individual and society, how to maintain authoritative structures of knowledge and moral conduct, how to overcome the breakdown of community and the pervasive alienation of the modern world.

ıey did not agree in their politics beyond that common ground. Comte, founder of 'positivism' (a word he coined along with 'sociology' and 'altruism') was a frank out-and-out authoritarian. In his *Catechism of Positive Religion*, he proclaims it his mission 'to deliver the West from an anarchical democracy and from a retrograde aristocracy, so to constitute, as far as practicable, a true Sociocracy, one combining wisely, in furtherance of the common regeneration, all the powers of man'.

Sociocracy, the rule of society, would in practice be implemented by bankers and industrialists, under the wise guidance of positivist priests. And it would be sustained by 'sociolatry', the worship of Society, the *Grand Être*: a collective entity made up of deserving human beings from all history.

We have seen what Mill thought of sociocracy. Nothing so politically *outré* is to be found in Hegel, which is one reason why his influence was eventually much greater. By the political standards of the time, Hegel was a conservative liberal. The state he favours is that unsuccessfully proposed by Prussian liberals in the 1810s and the 1820s, such men as Hardenberg and Wilhelm von Humboldt. It was by no means a democracy, but it had a constitutional monarch and a bicameral assembly.

Hegel gives an extended analysis of freedom; it is the ground theme of his whole philosophy, and it is important for the questions of this chapter. Freedom in his metaphysics is a category that actually applies more fundamentally and broadly than to the moral and political sphere alone. In that particular sphere, however, Hegel distinguishes three aspects of freedom. There is the liberty of the person enshrined in the rights of person, property and contract. There is the old idea of moral freedom as rational self-determination, in modern times expressed most clearly by Kant and associated with freedom of conscience and the right of moral self-governance. And then there is what Hegel calls objective (concrete, substantive) freedom. It is the freedom one reaches when one is not confronted by a limiting and alien social reality, but achieves insightful at-one-ness, reflective reconciliation, within a community that is and is seen to be rational. The first two of these kinds of freedom, liberty of the person and freedom of the moral subject, must, Hegel thinks, be inherent moments of modern objective freedom: the objective freedom towards which the modern world moves is a differentiated communal unity that preserves and completes them.

We have already seen, in the last two chapters, that the first two moments of Hegelian freedom are important elements in Mill's thinking. They correspond respectively to the rights of liberty and security that a modern society must respect, and to the personal quality of moral freedom or responsibility that forms one element in Mill's notion of self-development. It remains an important question what corresponds in Mill's thinking to Hegel's notion of objective freedom, and how they differ; for that lies at the heart of the difference between liberals and communitarians.

We should also compare Mill's thinking to that of the greatest left communitarian, Marx. Like the communitarians of the right, he too had a theory in which human history moves through necessary stages to a final collective goal. However, he did not think that the French revolutionary Terror revealed an inadequacy in the revolutionaries' understanding of freedom. True, they had acted without sufficient historical sense and needed a better understanding of the laws of motion of society. But whereas Hegel's idea of modern community encompasses the rights of person and property as an aspect of objective freedom, Marx thinks the very notion of rights should be overturned for the sake of objective freedom. Furthermore, where Hegel thinks that this objective freedom is possible only through citizenship in a rational state, Marx thinks it is possible only after the abolition of the state. Substantive freedom is possible only under communism, when rights and the liberal-bourgeois state that polices them have withered away.

Comte wanted an authoritarian positivist state, Hegel a constitutional State with a consultative assembly representing the estates of society, Marx wanted to get beyond the state altogether. And all of them were sufficiently historicist to think their preferred ideal of community was inevitable: the final outcome to which the modern world was destined by the laws of history.

What about the liberals? They too drew morals from the Terror and Bonapartism. They agreed that the revolutionaries lacked historical sense. The great lesson to learn from right-communitarian thinkers, Mill thought – he studied Comte as well as Coleridge – was the importance of social allegiance and historical continuity, and effective intellectual and moral authority in achieving that. In his essay on Coleridge, he agrees that the revolutionaries' error lay in insufficient appreciation of this and hence in 'attempting to new-model society without the binding forces which held society together' (X: 138). On the whole, however, what worried the liberals about democracy was not so much its potential for anarchy as its potential for a despotism exercised in the name of the people. It particularly worried French liberals such as Benjamin Constant, Mme de Staël and Alexis de Tocqueville. And it was a major impulse behind Mill's essay *On Liberty*, as we saw in the last chapter.

Democracy, the French liberals thought, was an inevitable expression of the modern notion of equality, and the modern notion of equality had to be accepted in principle. But they cherished civil liberty and suspected political liberty. Madame de Staël spoke for them when she said that the latter interests ambitious men who desire power, whereas the former interests peaceful men who do not want to be dominated.

That is not Mill's attitude; he is much keener on political liberty than that. He believed in the desirability, and eventual possibility, of equal participation in collective self-government.

He agrees that the dangers of modern politics will be those of conformism and loss of creativity, of individuals lost in the crowd and of centralising despotism: 'the only despotism of which in the modern world there is real danger – the absolute rule of the head of the executive over a congregation of isolated individuals, all equals but all slaves' (*Autobiography*, I: 201). But he thinks the antidote is to develop popular allegiance to liberal institutions: entrenched principles of individual liberty and free speech, and representative democracy. In a state of liberty under law there must be security of the person, but security may be detachable in some degree from rights of private property – Mill favoured experiments in socialism (4.3). So long as truly liberal institutions can focus allegiance and maintain participation, Mill optimistically thinks, democracy will avoid the various dangers of anarchy, despotism and mediocrity. Among liberals he was by some distance the keenest democrat, and this enthusiasm, as we shall see, was in fact connected with some at least of the ideas one associates with Hegel's 'objective freedom'.

The liberals were just as interested in history as Comte, Hegel and Marx; their historical vision is one thing that makes the early nineteenth century a classical moment for liberal thought. Furthermore, their philosophy of history, like that of Hegel and Marx, featured conflict as the motor of history. But there is an important difference. Whereas for Hegel and Marx the conflict (be it within forms of thought or between classes) was destined to come to an end with the arrival of modern community – a kind of 'end of history' – for the liberals conflict of interests and ideas was the permanent condition of progress. It was a basic liberal theme that conflict and dissent are functionally necessary features of a free and healthy society.

But the most fundamental disagreement between liberals and communitarians was, and continues to be, about the good for human beings. This is indeed basic, and we shall have to focus on it before our discussion is finished. For both sides, one can say, the central concept of the good is self-development, or in the more idealist phrase, self-realisation. German philosophy influentially identified freedom itself – positive or objective freedom – with self-realisation. The question then was what such freedom or self-realisation is, and by what social forms it is to be fostered. Is the overcoming of alienation essential to it, and is that possible only through some significant kind of at-one-ness with others and with the world itself? Left and right communitarians agree that it is. The question then is what modern form of community can bring this about. But while liberals can agree that freedom is self-realisation, the alleged problem of alienation, and consequent need for reconciliation within some modern form of community, are not for them significant. On the contrary, the crucial problem is how to preserve genuine, self-realising, individuality in an egalitarian and democratic state.

The right communitarian ideal is the ethic of service. It is expressed in contrasting ways in Hegel's concrete notion of individual self-realisation, constituted by embodiment in a network of role-duties ('The individual finds his liberation in duty') and in Comte's abstract idea of altruistic service to humanity. The liberal ideal of that time is more individualistic. There is, to be sure, complexity in this contrast. Mill, Humboldt or Schiller put a Periclean dimension of participation in public affairs into their ideal of harmoniously developed individuality (2.3). Hegel makes room for the private world of thought and feeling. Nonetheless there is real conflict here, a conflict that was to surface in later stages of liberalism. One thing that made Marx's communist vision so beguiling is the idea that under communism the two ideals – individuality and communal unity – will be combined (4.3). But most liberals treat such visions of dialectical unity with suspicion. It is not so easy to bring heaven down to earth.

The ideal of service, together with a certain ascetic-egalitarian ideal, did matter to Mill, even though they stand in some tension with the liberal ideal that mattered to him most of all. It is understandable that they mattered to him, because the former at least is truly attractive, while the latter has enduring charm to those who are dismayed by the way sheer luck rules the world. This is a preoccupation of moralists, and Mill is decidedly a moralist. But like other liberals Mill is not a theorist of alienation and reconciliation. For example, he notes that the 'social feelings of mankind' are strengthened by the much greater specialisation and interdependence of the modern world, and sees this as a good thing in so far as it provides a strengthening 'sanction' of utilitarian morality – but immediately goes on to worry that the motive of 'service of humanity' may become 'so excessive as to interfere unduly with human freedom and individuality' (X: 231ff.; *U* 3: 10).

Mill's encounter with Comte and the French liberals was direct; his encounter with German thinkers was largely indirect, coming initially at least through Coleridge and through friends influenced by German ideas. If he and Hegel are the two greatest moral and political thinkers of the nineteenth century, one can only think it a great pity that Mill never responded to Hegel directly. An extended exchange of views between them, of the kind that we have between Mill and Comte, would have been impossible – Hegel died when Mill was 15. But what one would give for a study by Mill of 'Hegel and Idealism' as thorough and thoughtful as his *Auguste Comte and Positivism* – especially in view of Hegel's subsequent influence, not just on Marxism but also on late nineteenth-century liberalism in Britain!

There are some striking similarities between them. They both have the ambition of reconciling Enlightenment and counter-Enlightenment insights. Mill thinks Bentham's utilitarianism brings ethics to a new level, in rather the way that Hegel thinks Kant's theory of morality as freedom does. Both are scathing, however, about the abstractness and narrowness of their respective mentors' insight into the subtlety and historical variability of human motives. Both are many-sided thinkers whose views are difficult to capture accurately. Both fight a battle on two fronts: against conservatives and against radical democrats. Mill mobilises his utilitarianism against people whom he sees as mere consecrators of the status quo – yet at other times he can sound like a Hegelian holist about shared customary morality, seeking only to criticise it from within. But the over-riding theme is unquestionably their respective views of freedom: in some ways so interestingly similar, yet at base so thoroughly different. Hegel was a conservative liberal in politics, but he was by no means philosophically a liberal. The difference lies in Mill's individualism, which we should now consider.

4.2 History and character

Mill discusses the 'logic of the moral sciences' in the *System of Logic*. It turns out that the moral science he is most interested in is historical sociology. On the importance of this new subject he strongly agreed with Comte; in fact, his ambitions for it were much greater than seems plausible now.

Maybe we have swung too far in the opposite direction. Historical sociology may not be able to produce anything worth calling laws in any strict sense, contrary to Mill's expectations; it does not follow that it cannot produce worthwhile explanatory tools. Historical ways of understanding the present are especially needed in crisis periods, such as Mill rightly took the early decades of the nineteenth century to be. The need is less felt in periods of stability, such as the forty or so years after the Second World War; in such times existing social forms come to seem indispensable and final. Now, however, with the collapse of European socialism, the convulsions of Islam, and the rise of questions about whether we are passing into a post-modernist age (questions which in many ways parallel those earlier questions about the 'modern age'), Mill's enthusiasm for historical sociology looks a lot more cogent.

But while he expected great things from historical sociology, he never doubted that its laws must fit into an individualist account of the moral sciences. Effusive as he is about Comte's foundational contributions to the subject, he completely rejects Comte's metaphysical holism, or collectivism, which the latter expresses with characteristic provocativeness:

> Man indeed, as an individual, cannot properly be said to exist, except in the too abstract brain of modern metaphysicians. Existence in the true sense can only be predicated of Humanity.

Contrast Mill:

> Men ... in a state of society, are still men; their actions and passions are obedient to the laws of individual human nature ... Human beings in society have no properties but those which are derived from, and may be resolved into, the laws of the nature of individual man.
>
> (VIII: 879)

Historical sociology may have its laws, but they are not the laws of some supra-individual subject, be it Society, Spirit, or Humanity. Mill's detailed analysis of the moral sciences (which occupies the whole of Book VI of his *System of Logic*) is a classic exposition of individualism. It has a robust realism and analytic clarity that communitarian metaphysical effusions wholly lack. At the same time, its emphasis on historical and sociological understanding is a great gain for liberal theory in Britain, which always seems to suffer from a tendency to draw simple-minded deductions about society and politics from supposed axioms about individual human behaviour.

That granted, did Mill's belief in the historical and social mutability of human character go too far? Although this doctrine of mutability is very much part of his nineteenth-century side, he in fact bases it on a theory that he inherits from the Enlightenment – associationism. Associationism says that there are no innate differences of psychology between human beings; similarities and differences of individual mental disposition all result from laws of psychological association working on similarities and differences of environment. In his more cautious moments Mill accepted that this was a hypothesis that might turn out to be wrong. But it was a hypothesis that mattered to him greatly. It removed the notion that differences of character and intelligence across individuals, races or nations are fixed and indelible; it gave him a basis for the belief that human nature is historically changeable and – in favourable social conditions – progressive. It thus provided the bridge between what Mill knew to be possible in the actual state of human society and character, and what he thought might be achieved if only we could trigger a virtuous spiral of interactions between improving states of society and improving states of character. It allowed him, in other words, to combine horse sense about the present with conditional utopianism about the future.

The desired future was a free and equal society in which people develop their all-round human potential: the liberal ideal, with its Schillerian roots (2.3). But isn't there a problem in combining this with associationism? The liberal ideal relies on the idea that individuals have naturally determinate potentials, that they flourish insofar as those potentials are realised, and that good forms of social life produce deeper or finer forms of happiness because they permit these natural dispositions of thought and feeling to flourish. This is implicit in the idea of spontaneity. Determinate human nature grounds objective human interests and provides the benchmark for ethical principles and political institutions.

The German tradition, Aristotelian and Hegelian, offered an explicitly teleological anthropology in which to cast this view. Is this Aristotelian and Hegelian inheritance indispensable? What does Mill need to ground the notion of real interests?

He needs the notion of a natural or spontaneous disposition and the idea that human beings achieve fullest satisfaction, the life of greatest well-being, when those natural dispositions are fully expressed. He can then distinguish between external conditions which impede or distort this natural flowering and conditions which facilitate it. But one might expect an associationist to deny that there are such natural dispositions (whether in ethics or in epistemology). Should he not hold that human nature is educable into whatever dispositions general utility requires? A small initial class of actions is instinctively pleasant or painful, but there is no limit to what can be associated with pleasure or pain from that narrow base. Shouldn't this malleability of human character mean that character, as well as institutions and means of production, become variables in the equation which the utilitarian policy-maker tries to solve for greatest utility? For example, making people more altruistic should be possible, and of course Mill did want a society in which the good of others was much more a part of each person's good. But the Millian emphasis, that liberty is founded on human potentiality, has no obvious role. It looks as though the combination of hedonism and associationism would more naturally lead to those dystopian brave new worlds we have all learned to fear.

However, this does not follow strictly from associationism. Mill distinguishes between 'natural' and 'innate'. What matters for epistemology and ethics is the natural or spontaneous disposition of thought, feeling, or will as against the artificial or imposed one. It's possible that there are associations that are natural, that is, historically and socially invariant, and that these are enough to underwrite the determinate-potentialities view of human nature Mill works with in his ethical and political theory. Furthermore, the differences of association that underlie people's different potentialities might result from interactions with their physiology, pre-natal experiences, specific non-social experiences, etc. in ways that no counter-association could erase. What is less legitimate, in view of this point, is the way Mill uses associationism as a battering ram against intuitionism in ethics and epistemology, and as a security for his strong belief in human equality and unlimited improveability. He himself has to appeal to reflectively known natural dispositions in his ethics and epistemology. As to the theses of equality and improveability, the most he should say is that associationism gives hope that they may be true.

Associationism is no longer the dominant psychological paradigm. In practice, in any case, Mill works with the determinate-potentialities picture. It underlies his discussion of individuality in *On Liberty*, and his account of the higher pleasures in *Utilitarianism;* it can be found in many other places too. He emphasizes the diversity of natural endowments and therefore the diversity of forms of good life but he thinks there are also common features in the good life for all human beings. That is implicit, for example, in Mill's conception of the virtues as a part or ingredient of the truly happy life. Generosity, nobility of feeling, honesty and humanity in personal relations, moral courage, rationality – these are qualities which Mill admires. He holds that they are outgrowths of natural human propensities – they appear in thought and feeling as natural ideals – and a normal human being who lacks them senses their lack and feels the poorer for it. That optimistic theme is an important part of Mill's construction of liberalism on a utilitarian base. Historical sociology gives him confidence: it tells him that failure to understand historical continuity explains revolutionary disaster, while failure to understand historical progress explains conservative pessimism. He shares with Marx the conviction that men make history even as history makes men.

4.3 Marx and Mill on the good for human beings

Marx's intellectual development, however, went in the opposite direction to Mill's. Mill was educated in his teens as a democrat, legal rationaliser and classical political economist. He had a thorough grounding in the utilitarian arguments for modern liberal society. In political economy they implied free competition between independent risk-takers, in jurisprudence, rights of person and property entrenched by clearly codified law, in politics, democratic government responsive to the interests of all. He found a firm footing on that solid Anglo-Scottish platform; only afterwards did he begin to experience the predicaments of modern people to which it seemed to him his teachers had been blind, and which must somehow transform, though not destroy, the simple virtues of their system. Marx (born 12 years after Mill) started from a German intellectual milieu in which precisely these ethical or spiritual preoccupations were to the fore. While at university in his teens he studied Kant and Fichte and became immersed in Hegel. Then in his twenties, he studied Anglo-Scottish political economy, and undertook to rethink it within the speculative project of a historical materialism derived from 'turning Hegel right side up'.

This project makes Marx one of the great historical sociologists. That thought-forms are the outcome of productive material activity by determinate human beings; that history develops through successive contradictions between forces and relations of production: these are seminal ideas for social science. But Marx's historical sociology also subserves an ethical vision of a world to come, a world of liberated human powers and community. History is progress towards the final goal of human emancipation, in which we shall realise our true nature by freely producing for the benefit of each other:

In the individual expression of my life I will have directly created your expression of your life, and therefore in my individual activity I will have directly *confirmed* and *realised* my true nature, my *human* nature, my *communal* nature.

As I mentioned earlier, Marx's vision of communism combines communitarian and liberal ideals. Human beings will achieve complete ethical at-one-ness, overcoming their estrangement from themselves and from each other. At the same time, each will fully and freely develop all the potential powers of his or her distinctive individuality. Communist society will be 'the only society in which the genuine and free development of individuals ceases to be a mere phrase'.

Communism will abolish all distinctions between public and private life, general and particular interests; it will therefore abolish private property, money, and the state itself, for the state 'is based on the contradiction between *public* and *private* life, on the contradiction between *general interests* and *private interests'*. Marx thinks that truly political debate about conflicting ideals or interests, as against administration of the common good, can simply go away. The excuse for this outrageous failure to think clearly and sensibly about communism is borrowed from Hegel: detailed thinking about the dialectical outcome of history is impossible as well as redundant. What dialectics tells us is only that communism will satisfy all aspirations and abolish all tensions – and that it is inevitable. Or as one might unsympathetically put it, who thinks clearly and sensibly about paradise?

By comparison to Marx's fervour, Mill's experimental attitude to socialism, though it does not lack moral passion, is a much more sceptical affair. The difference is partly that between a prophet and an empiricist, but there is also a difference of ideals – a fascinating one, because they are in some ways close. In his

Autobiography, Mill says that he gradually became more of a 'qualified' socialist and less of a 'pure' democrat (I: 199). We'll consider what he means about becoming a less pure democrat in the next section. What about his socialism?

It is certainly qualified. Mill sides strongly with socialists in their criticism of the capitalism he knew: its mass poverty, wage-slavery, and glaring disproportion 'between success and merit, or between success and exertion' (V: 714). But he is wary of comparing capitalism as it actually is with socialism as it is dreamed it might be. When it comes to sober assessment, especially in the unfinished and posthumously published 'Chapters on Socialism', a very cautious reckoning emerges.

Capitalism is not doomed by the laws of history:

> The present system is not, as many Socialists believe, hurrying us into a state of general indigence and slavery from which only Socialism can save us. The evils and injustices suffered under the present system are great, but they are not increasing; on the contrary, the general tendency is towards their slow diminution.
>
> (V: 736)

Nor is it unjust to allow capital to extract profit from labour: a rate of profit for capital is justified by the abstention and risk undertaken by its owners. Furthermore, socialists make a basic mistake in criticising competition. It is in general beneficial, and abuses such as culpable bankruptcy and fraud can be checked by good law. Where the nature of the product restricts market competition to a small number of large enterprises, production can be regulated or taken over by the state. Overall, there still remains a lot of room for improvement within the capitalist system. Profit-sharing schemes for workers could be introduced. Land could be declared the property of the state without interfering with the right of property in anything that is the product of human labour and abstinence. Inheritance taxes could be set to eliminate any unearned fortune within a few generations.

Revolutionary socialists attract Mill's strong hostility, as we might by now expect. They are ready to destroy people's existing securities for the sake of a new social system that no-one has tested – showing 'a serene confidence in their own wisdom on the one hand and a recklessness of other people's sufferings on the other, which Robespierre and St. Just, hitherto the typical instances of those united attributes, scarcely came up to' (V: 737). Equally objectionable is their centralising tendency. Since directing the whole economy from a single centre is impossible, a centralising takeover would be likely to devolve rapidly to unskilled and uneducated hands; if the whole system then came under the regulation of a state bureaucracy, freedom would exist only in name.

But there is another way. Socialism can be introduced experimentally in small-scale trials. The form of socialism Mill thinks most promising is a system of competing producer co-operatives. He sees difficulties, however, in socialist systems of remuneration: it is the familiar problem of what incentive they provide for exertion. The communist ideal is that work is done for the common good. The 'one certainty' is that that requires a high level of moral and intellectual education for everyone in the community (V: 746). Mill by no means excludes the long-term possibility of such education; this is one notable place where his faith in the historical progressiveness of human nature comes to his aid:

Education, habit, and the cultivation of the sentiments will make a common man dig or weave for his country, as readily as fight for his country. True enough, it is only by slow degrees, and a system of culture prolonged through successive generations, that men in general can be brought up to this point. But the hindrance is not in the essential constitution of human nature. Interest in the common good is at present so weak a motive in the generality not because it can never be otherwise, but because the mind is not accustomed to dwell on it as it dwells from morning till night on things which tend only to personal advantage. When called into activity, as only self-interest now is, by the daily course of life, and spurred from behind by the love of distinction and the fear of shame, it is capable of producing, even in common men, the most strenuous exertions as well as the most heroic sacrifices.

(I: 239–41)

So Mill thinks that the collaborative pursuit of common good may be a realistic ultimate human goal, but he also sees the dangers of a less favourable outcome. If the incentive is not money, it can come to be status and power. Furthermore, collective decision would have to take over where individual decision is better – he takes the education of children as an example. All this flows into the crucial Millian question: how well would such a system preserve individuality? Wouldn't communism compress individuality and impose conformism to an unprecedented degree?

This assessment of the risks is very shrewd. Nonetheless, Mill is clearly stirred by communist ideals. His presentation of the possibility of a society running on public spirit, however 'ultimate' a prospect it may be, smacks of wishful thinking, as even the prose of the just quoted passage betrays. In national emergencies, people may be willing to die for their country, and to dig and weave for their country. Can they ever be expected to get on with the humdrum business of normal life for their country – for the general good? Public spirit emerges impressively in emergencies, and in certain public aspects of life, but is it possible for it to be the general motive of everyday life? Is that even desirable, given the importance to liberalism of the division between public and private? Shouldn't Mill have remembered his criticisms of Comte's altruism at this point?

He does not think socialist systems have an efficiency advantage over capitalist systems, or that they have an inherent justice advantage over capitalist systems. On the one hand, the socialist system that he thinks may work, of freely competing workers' co-operatives, preserves the utility of competition but also leaves some of these co-operatives to flourish and others to go out of business; on the other, the reforms of capitalism that he advocates would diminish the disproportions between deserts and reward that he dislikes. They would not eliminate them entirely, but then neither would the system of competing co-operatives.

It seems then that for him the distinctive ethical attraction of socialism, if it could work, is indeed the communitarian ideal of working together for the common good. We can split this in turn into two ideas

1 Socialism requires the virtue of public spirit.
2 It is intrinsically self-realising to work for each other.

(1) is perfectly correct but not an argument for socialism. Virtue is admirable, but that does not imply that we should try to bring about situations in which it is needed. For example, courage in the face of serious danger, or the capacity to sacrifice oneself for a noble cause, are great virtues. That doesn't mean that we should proliferate situations of serious danger, or causes that require great self-sacrifice. So even though Mill rightly admires public spirit, and sees that it is required to make socialism work, the point must be not (1) but (2) – not that socialism requires great virtues to work at all, but that it is an intrinsically good, satisfying, desirable, way

to live. It must be that working together for the common good is a higher pleasure. So the question is to what extent that is true.

A down-to-earth answer is that this is indeed a fulfilling way to live – to many people for some of the time, and to some people for much of the time. But what most people mostly want is to pursue their own projects. Working together for the common good is a noble ideal but it is only one ideal. For most people it is the private preoccupations of individual life that supply the overwhelmingly large portion of well-being. If the question was put squarely to Mill, that would surely be his answer too. And he is well aware of the danger of trying to impose socialist ideals of living on those who don't want them.

The really perilous Marxist notion, from a liberal standpoint, is the notion that conflict between particular and general interests can be somehow abolished. In its extreme, and in one way most attractive form, the left-communitarian ideal envisages a self-transparent collective subject pursuing a common good in a conflict-free, and hence justice-free, way. The general will prevails, the rest is mere administration of things. It is a cornerstone of any liberalism that this cannot be. There is no collective subject; there are individual subjects who have common interests but also diverging, and often competing, ones. Justice is indispensable to this situation, and the state is indispensable as the guarantor of justice.

Mill always agreed with the older generation of utilitarians about the importance of a system of justice that guarantees security (2.5). He has a favourable rather than a hostile attitude to the 'bourgeois' politics of interest adjustment. What is that, at its best, other than just compromise? Just compromise is the essence of civil society. So the political is not something that can disappear. Nor is it merely a means of finding a *modus vivendi*: the compromise should be just. The political process is a moral process, and valuable in itself, for political virtues are a part of self-development and thus of happiness. It is in fact the virtues of democratic citizenship, rather than the virtues of 'socialist man', that best realise Mill's liberal ideal.

4.4 Democracy

If Mill's assessment of socialism is pretty much in line with what many politically thoughtful people have come to believe, that is not the case with his assessment of democracy. Rightly or wrongly, he is probably both more enthusiastic about its potential for making people better, and more worried about its capacity to make people worse, than most people who actually live in democracies now are.

Some of his proposals line up with common liberal-democratic views today: he favours decentralisation, proportional representation, and he was throughout his life an active worker for the enfranchisement of women, at a time when that was still controversial. Others are strikingly out of line: he thinks that votes should be cast in public, that those with higher education should have more votes, while those who cannot read, write or do simple arithmetic, or who pay no taxes, should have no votes at all. (The last restriction is based on the very dubious principle that representation should be co-extensive with taxation.) Yet by the standards of his own time, Mill was a committed democrat, though even then a decidedly quirky one.

Under the quirkiness is a consistency of view. Mill is elitist along two distinct tracks – first, about things that require technical or managerial skill and, second, about moral or cultural distinction. But he is strongly egalitarian, in principle, about political discussion and decision. Since both the executive business of government and the drafting of laws require ability and specialised knowledge, he concludes that these should not be done directly by the assembly of democratically elected representatives. The assembly should above all deliberate; it should determine policy and control its execution, but not execute it. It should instruct a specially constituted commission of experts to draft legislation according to its policy wishes, but it would ordinarily be expected not to make its own amendments, though it could send back drafts to the commission. Likewise, it should in some way effectively decide who the prime minister, or head of the executive, should be, but should then leave other appointments to him or her. As to the question of creativity in moral and cultural matters, that raises different issues, concerning the limits of popular sovereignty, which we have already discussed. Groundbreaking activity in these fields is the province of the few, Mill thinks, and the main thing is to ensure conditions of liberty which leave them, along with everyone else, free to pursue their projects and to seek to persuade others to follow their lead.

Political deliberation and decision, however, concern the pursuit of public good, determination of collective duty, and just adjudication among conflicting interests. What these require is not technical expertise or creative insight but virtue and good sense. (Eloquence helps, and was a subject Mill took seriously.) Everyone, Mill thinks, has the ability to take up civic duties in a responsible way. It is legitimate to demand from everyone, and imperative to foster, civic responsibility. Thus it is not unreasonable to require that voting be public, since the vote exercises a public trust, not a private right. (Mill does not overlook the danger of bribery and intimidation; the antidote he romantically relies on is rectitude and courage.) In contrast, however, so long as the education of citizens, as against their technical training, remains poor those with greater education must have greater political influence.

Mill's urgent anxieties about the conformist and mediocritising tendencies of democracy (3.3) are important – it's equally important that his ethics supplies democracy with very solid supporting pillars. A utilitarian, of course, must hold that the 'the test of what is right in politics is not the *will* of the people, but the *good* of the people' (XXIII: 502). So Mill does not belong to the tradition that bases popular sovereignty, any more than liberty, on what he would call 'abstract right'. He does not think democracy is always the best system, and even in sufficiently advanced conditions in which it is the best system, it is still justly constrained by principles of liberty. He remains a liberal first and a democrat second; nonetheless, over all matters legitimately decidable by politics, he thinks the people as a whole must take control. 'Modern nations will have to learn the lesson, that the well-being of a people must exist by means of the justice and self-government ... of the individual citizens' (III: 763).

The traditional utilitarian argument for this conclusion, and a good one, is that people's interests can only be securely represented through votes, because no-one else knows them better, or is likely more zealously to promote them. Mill fully accepts that argument, but puts it into his usual historical, developmental context. Further, he sees the value of democracy in less instrumental terms. The best government in general is that which best and most effectively improves the people, and democracy is best at improving a sufficiently advanced people. This standpoint separates him both from the more instrumental arguments from democracy and from those liberals of today who think that the state should not be involved in people's conceptions of the good (5.4). For Mill thinks that the state should be actively seeking to *improve* people. 'The first element of good government [is] the virtue and intelligence of the human beings composing the community', and

> the most important point of excellence which any form
> of government can possess is to promote the virtue and

intelligence of the people themselves. The first question in respect to any political institutions is, how far they tend to foster in the members of the community the various desirable qualities, moral and intellectual; or rather (following Bentham's more complete classification) moral, intellectual, and active.

(XIX: 390)

When a nation has not advanced to the stage at which democratic self-government becomes viable, the best government for it is a benevolent autocracy genuinely dedicated to guiding it forward to that stage. (The idea is beloved by an unsavoury crew of military dictators, but that does not make it wrong.) That, Mill thought, provided a temporary justification for the East India Company's rule over India. He was one of its senior officials, and defended it to Parliament in 1858 against the proposal that the British state should take over its role. His argument was that the Company was more genuinely dedicated to advancing India towards self-government than the British state would be. He did not carry the day.

Education in virtue and intelligence is one necessary condition of representative government. National solidarity is another:

when a people are ripe for free institutions, there is a still more vital consideration. Free institutions are next to impossible in a country made up of different nationalities. Among a people without fellow-feeling, especially if they read and speak different languages, the united public opinion, necessary for the working of representative government, cannot exist.

(XIX: 547)

There can be federations of nations if there is sufficient common interest, but representative government requires national solidarity as well as individual virtue. Without both of these there can be no civil society; without civil society there can be no representative government. Mill is a liberal nationalist not a liberal cosmopolitan. His reasons come back again to historical sociology. He endorses the counter-Enlightenment emphasis on the significance of origin, allegiance and becoming. Not that he takes this as far as German philosophical nationalism took it; he does not see nations as collective embodiments of Spirit acting in world history, and he is a civic not an ethnic nationalist.

Hegel was not a democrat, a liberal or a utilitarian. Yet the terms by which Mill judges the viability and value of democracy would have been somewhat congenial to him. For both philosophers the primary question is what effect a form of government has on the excellence of citizens. Involvement in public affairs at any level, Mill thinks, brings responsibility, public spirit, independence, and thus self-development. Whether or not we call this idea 'objective freedom', the point is that in adding democratic participation to it Mill takes it further in its natural direction. He and Hegel would also have agreed that a good state requires a common culture; the difference between them is that Mill emphasises democracy and diversity while Hegel emphasises common culture. Again, the features of democracy that Hegel feared were those that Mill also feared: dominance of sectional interests, openness to demagoguery, the danger of atomised individuals lost in crowds and feeling and thinking in crowds. In response to these dangers, Hegel puts his trust in social units – the family, the corporation, the estate – whereas Mill continues to put his trust in individuals. Some aspects of this contrast have been illustrated; it could be illustrated further, for example, by contrasting their views on marriage. For Hegel, the married couple is a paradigmatically communal unit, a unity-in-difference with a reproductive social mission. For Mill, it is a companionate relationship – though these companions have weighty civic responsibilities to consider if they think of having children (3.2).

Mill puts his heart into democracy because democracy fulfils his ideal of active, invigorating freedom. There are many ways of being truly *individual*. But one very good way is to be a conscientious, independent member of the nation's democratic assembly, elected by a system of voting that gives all interests and opinions their proportionate weight, listening to the deliberations of the assembly and the people, deciding from your conscience. A representative individual, not a mere delegate of any social group.

5

Reflection

————•◆•————

We now have a picture of Mill's answers to the questions posed at the beginning – how to live, how to live together. Let us reflect on it. Certainly, Mill sets out a real option. It is not a set of high-minded platitudes that no-one could dispute; nor is it an outlook that we might find interestingly strange but could not think of adopting. It is close enough, but different enough, to current attitudes to be challenging. He develops a liberal, humanistic and civic ideal which stands in distinct contrast to other visions, such as the soul-saving ascetic ideal provided by the great religious faiths, the ideal of reconciliation and service to others provided by communitarian ideals of society, and strange as it may seem to pick out a single thinker in this context, the anti-political aesthetic perfectionism of Nietzsche. These are contrasts between ultimate convictions, but that does not mean they cannot be debated – does any debate matter more? We can think freely about them. We can examine the philosophical and empirical tenets on which they rest. To be sure, free thought itself, as noted in Chapter 1, is a contested concept. It is not acknowledged as a neutral umpire by all parties. Some think there are other ultimate sources of normative authority, others think there is no normative authority. That does not mean they are right. Mill starts from the contested, but correct, view that free thought has adequate authority for the task and nothing else does. He rightly thinks that his method of thinking from within (1.3) is a virtuous spiral, not a vicious circle.

5.1 Mill as a late-modern thinker

Compared to Hegel and Marx, Mill stands out as an individualist. It is a very big difference yet also a subtle one. We have laid out some of its aspects in Chapter 4. Mill is just as historical as they are, just as concerned to diagnose modernity and identify its distinctive demands. Like them, he thinks of natural rights and social contracts as early-modern fictions – so that is a classic kind of individualism that he does not endorse. Crucially, however, he shares neither their holistic social metaphysics nor their sense that alienation is a fundamental modern problem. Undoubtedly he is deeply interested, like most other thinkers after the French Revolution, in the binding forces that hold a society together. Nationality, citizenship and patriotism are important concepts for him, not only in social explanation but also as significant ethical categories. However, we have seen that this emphasis on civic allegiance falls well short of truly communitarian ideals. Democratic citizenship is for Mill an important forum for developing and exercising individual moral responsibility. He believes in representation of and by individual citizens; his basic interest is not that 'vague abstraction, the good of the country, but the actual, positive well-being of the living human creatures who compose the population' (XVIII: 67). The communist ideal somewhat enthuses Mill in the abstract, but when he thinks more concretely about it he soon starts to worry that it will impose bureaucracy and undermine individuality. Neither Hegel's corporate state nor Marx's stateless community represent his ideal of civic and individual life.

We can think of the period beginning with the French Revolution and ending with the decline of 'actually existing' socialism in the years through to 1989 as late-modern, in that in some unclear yet important sense we are now post-modern; though what this means we don't yet know. At any rate, in several ways, the most telling comparison now is no longer between Mill and Hegel and Marx but between Mill and Nietzsche.

They have one major thing in common: a passion for human greatness and a real fear of modern mediocrity. But Nietzsche vehemently rejects the very foundations of the late-modern stance. In doing so, he rejects two things that greatly matter to Mill:

1   self-development, as against voluntaristic self-making;
2   impartiality and equality.

Nietzsche rejects them because he rejects objectivity. He believes neither in a self with determinate potential, nor in an objective framework by reference to which self-development can be said to be progressive or degenerative. He further thinks all doctrines of equality are a hangover of Christian 'slave-morality', as is the desire for truth itself.

Go back to our contrast between two conceptions of free thought (1.2). Nietzsche stands in the tradition that takes it that free thought must be presuppositionless thought. He also sees that if free thought cannot provide normative authority, neither can fideistic apologetics, or appeal to a platonic realm of Reason; and he sees German idealism's failure to deal with the resulting problem. He concludes that free thought (which he sees as itself a historical thing, a product of the Christian value placed on truthfulness and conscience) is the final step to nihilism. Nietzsche neither embraces nor exactly rejects nihilism: what he thinks is that he is the first to have seen that European culture is heading for it and that new values must be created in response, not through the pretence of objectivity, or appeal to a religious or metaphysical 'Beyond', but through an affirmation of the will. In other words, the denial of objectivity becomes in Nietzsche's hands a basic existential issue. And this has become, with the time lags by which culture sometimes follows philosophy, hugely influential.

If one is dazzled by it, it comes as a surprise and an anti-climax to find that Mill simply sees no 'problem' of objectivity. He is firmly established in the alternative tradition that takes free thought to be unconstrained rather than presuppositionless. Instead of grappling heroically with scepticism, he mildly emphasises fallibilism: taking it for granted that the methods of thinking from within – critical reflection on our inherited convictions, free discussion, the appeal to reflectively endorsed dispositions – are available and satisfactory. To use a well-established metaphor, he sees free thought as a ship on an open ocean. Any part can come to need repair, but we always have to rely on other parts to make the repair. So there is no crisis of scepticism, but there is an important task of improving and refining our methods in science and ethics.

Suppose we agree with Mill's confidence that free thought delivers normative objectivity. Then we might wonder why that kind of confidence collapses so spectacularly in the twentieth century, at least in politics and the humanities.

The collapse is manifest in a wide range of symptoms. Existentialism is one of them: it is the attempt to extract a super-value, an inspiring self-image, out of the very assertion of nihilism about values. In Nietzsche's version it is the glamorous dream of remaking a new aristocratic ethics after Christianity. Drabber, but far more wide-spread as a symptom, is the assertion of purely 'means–end' conceptions of rationality, with more-or-less obviously fallacious attempts to base ethical and political principles on that. Nihilism has an exhilarating Romantic variant and a plodding philistine variant; either way it is irreconcilable with the humanistic content of classical liberalism.

So what causes it? Important as philosophy may be, it would be foolish to think that the sole causes are mistakes in philosophy. No doubt there are many answers. There is the ebbing of religious faith, the pressure on the normative exercised by the dominance of science and consequent scientistic models of objectivity (these are not the fault of science, of course). But might not part of the answer be that questioning of objectivity is itself a characteristic effect of democracy? Objectivism, especially in ethics and the arts, is felt as elitism. And a typical response to elitism about such values is a sense of humiliation and an angry assertion of equal worth. Nietzsche would have recognised that, though he would have hated its upshot: that his own view, popularised, becomes a characteristic form of democratic self-delusion and a refuge for popular mediocrity.

5.2 *Culture and democracy*

I have quoted Mill's description of *On Liberty* as 'a kind of philosophic textbook of a single truth' (p. 52). Its lesson, he conceded, might seem unnecessary in a period 'decidedly favourable to the development of new opinions'. But he thought his time was a time of transition, with the openness of such times. With the settling in of a democratic and equal state, orthodoxies suiting that state would come to dominate social opinion. 'It is then that the teachings of the *Liberty* will have their greatest value' (I: 260).

What Mill feared from democracy was majoritarian despotism and conformist mediocrity. What he hoped was that it would be the greatest school of self-governance. He was *both* a moral and cultural elitist *and* an optimistic political and civic egalitarian.

That is a very good starting point for assessing democracy. Was he too pessimistic about its drift to mediocrity? Too optimistic about its potential for developing the virtue of self-governance?

The first question breaks down into two parts. Is there a decline of spiritual and aesthetic greatness in modern democracies, and a destruction of genuine individuality? If so, is democracy itself the cause?

We must fix more clearly where the worry lies. It is not a problem of morality or intellect. Any liberal must count the softening of traditional moral ferocity, the elimination of sheer moral prejudice and irrational taboo, as a great gain for the human spirit. This can be gladly acknowledged even by liberals who see the urgency of pulling back from 'liberalism' in the current non-philosophical sense of 'permissiveness', and of reasserting that individual moral responsibility is central to liberalism properly understood.

Similar remarks apply to the intellectual domain of science and scholarship. They are at unparalleled levels of development and support. Maybe here some worries about mediocritisation and conformism begin to seep in. Still these collective activities continue solidly, and in doing so, underpin rationality steadily – which is their pre-eminent indirect social function.

The crisis is rather one of ethical and aesthetic self-identity. The problem is the coarsening or diminution of ideals of the good. It is a problem of our art, our ideals, our aspirations for our own improvement as human beings, not of our cognitive inquiries or moral commitment. We lack powerful and inspiring models, whether in art or philosophy, of a life worth living. So much recent art seems to fall on a spectrum between inner exile and vacuous gimmickry. It can be grandly, gloomily vacuous, playfully, self-consciously vacuous, posturingly, 'subversively' vacuous, or just fatuous. This looks like the 'weariness' that Nietzsche thought would afflict modern life.

But for all we know it is temporary. We are at the end of the modernist and socialist century. Its first half was both a period of unimaginable political savagery and a period of extraordinary aesthetic renewal. It is not surprising if what follows that is a time of exhaustion. Furthermore, because of these upheavals, we are hardly well supplied with data to test the idea that peaceful and prosperous liberal democratic states destroy individuality. Perhaps only with the end of cold war and the collapse of the socialist model have we reached the right conditions for testing it.

And if the cause of our aesthetic and spiritual impoverishment is something more permanent, it needn't be democracy. Is it the decline of faith? Can modern humanist ideals, including Mill's, be sufficiently inspiring to sustain great art? Or is modern specialism the problem (a worry that goes back to Schiller)? Is the economic and intellectual specialisation that modern society absolutely requires reconcilable with the liberal ideal of harmonious all-round development? Or, again, is the cause of our spiritual diminishment capitalism, and the dominance it gives to con-tractual and commercial relations? All these hypotheses have been proposed.

Yet capitalism, specialisation and the decline of faith have been around for a long time now. It would be sheer complacency to rule out the worrying hypothesis that democracy itself has an inbuilt populist drift, which eventually cuts down all great and serious ideals to a 'tolerant' equality of standing, removes public and objective acknowledgement of their grandeur, and instead reinforces only those emotions strongly felt by the many. The liberal ideal itself degrades to a glib emancipationism: a con-formist, phoney-independent self-image for the hip consumer.

Hugely healthy, in face of these depressing thoughts, is Mill's and Nietzsche's intransigent refusal to compromise on aesthetic and moral excellence. Yet in Nietzsche's case, given his assault on objectivity, it looks like arbitrary stubbornness. Whence come the standards of excellence? They have to be wilfully created and imposed by supermen. Nothing in Nietzsche's philosophy offers a way out of this spectacular dead end.

But then are Mill's remedies enough? On his view, standards are immanently discovered (discovered 'from within') through free dialogue. Free dialogue goes on naturally, and is naturally influential – so long as liberty is protected – and liberty is protected by active political participation and resistance to populist pressures. That may all look a bit limp, or emptily optimistic, to anyone who is really anguished by modern vacuousness, as Nietzsche was. But is there another way of sustaining truly serious culture and a truly liberal ideal of individual development? The facts of twentieth-century history, it is often said, must undermine the nineteenth century's belief in progress. So what are we supposed to feel instead: a greater anxiety about democracy than Mill's? No-one, as a matter of fact, is seriously proposing an alternative. The antidote to democracy's dangers had better come from within democracy.

5.3 *Equality*

What, next, of the doctrines of equality that are so important to Mill, and that Nietzsche scorns? On what resilient natural dispositions can Mill base them? In particular, what disposition grounds impartiality?

This was a gap in Mill's 'proof' of the principle of utility (2.2). The question he should have answered, and did not, is why the criterion of conduct should be the well-being of all, impartially considered, rather than being for each person, *that* person's good, together with the good of such others as matter to him or her.

Well, we do think that no-one's well-being is more important than anyone else's, and this seems as resilient and natural a disposition as any. Of course, the well-being of *your* children, say, matters more to you than the well-being of some other children you don't even know. But you're very unlikely to express that personal commitment by saying that your children's well-being just is more important, *absolutely*, than those other children's. You don't hold that your children's well-being has a greater value that everyone else should acknowledge. That would plainly be unreasonable. Of course, one could agree with that while denying that *anyone's* well-being has 'absolute' value. So Mill needs a further disposition, a disposition to think that each person's well-being does indeed have absolute value.

This disposition too we have. It is rooted not in desire but in good will. Since Mill distinguishes between desire and will (2.3) he can agree with that. He might accept, in a certain *rapprochement* to Kant, that *impartiality* is the disposition that the will is left with when it abstracts from all desire. This would give impartiality the right authority. He would then need to explain how the disposition to impartiality gets in there on his own story about the evolution of the will. And that, given his associationist psychology, looks difficult. But that may be a problem for Mill's associationism, rather than a problem for the good will and its disposition of impartiality.

I don't think Nietzsche's critique of Christianity has much destructive purchase on this fundamental disposition of impartiality. It is too deep to be seen as a Christian hangover. But we have ideas about equality that go beyond mere impartiality. What of the notion that well-being should match desert? Or the doctrine of the equal dignity and worth of persons? These too had some importance for Mill.

Nietzsche's subversive claim that these ideas are products of Christian slave-morality looks more powerful. And it should be taken seriously by Mill's own epistemological standards. For what Nietzsche is saying is that without the intervention of a slave-morality based on *ressentiment*, the ideas that well-being should match desert, or that everyone has equal worth, seems *unnatural* rather than natural. Without the Christian narrative, in which we are all equally loved but tested children of God, it loses its normative authority. Likewise with Nietzsche's critique of egalitarianism, which he sees as an ascetic ideal that expresses the will to power of the weak.

His critique of these ideas is stronger because they start off weaker anyway. The idea that well-being should track desert generalises desert from those contexts in which it securely belongs – such as justice in punishment, or justice in honours and praise, or fairness in rewards for contribution to a collective task – to the whole of life: the divergent lives and fortunes of distinct individuals who are not engaged in a common task. Similarly, even if we accept, contra Nietzsche, that the ideal of an ascetic community living in shared material equality is genuinely attractive, and not a mere expression of the will to power, it still remains only an ideal. It is not a moral requirement to be imposed on everyone.

True, the whole of life *is* subject to fairness if God has set us all a common task. It is then up to Him to reward us fairly. Or if we accept a communitarianism that says we naturally own all our resources in common, including the talents and virtues of individuals, well, then we must divide the fruits of our joint labour fairly. But these ideas about fairness, desert and equality do not flow from Mill's utilitarian starting point (though he was clearly attracted by them in any case). All that philosophical utilitarianism says is that every individual's well-being has absolute value, and that this value must be counted impartially in assessing overall good. That, as we noted above (2.2), leaves the distributive structure of overall good open: which among many possible impartial functions from individual well-being to overall good should we endorse? The classical utilitarians' sum-total criterion is only one option, and an unattractive one. It does have the attraction of simplicity, but then subsequent discussion has made it ever more evident that a simple answer to this particular question is precisely what we will not find.

What about the doctrine of equal worth – does that fall under Nietzsche's critique? This is more complex. Equal respect is not the same as impartial concern. Impartial concern says that in assessing the overall goodness or badness of consequences we should take the impact on everyone's well-being into account impartially. Respect, on the other hand, refers to a person's standing, worth or dignity, and the doctrine of equal respect says that everyone has equal standing, worth or dignity. Impartial concern requires no doctrine of equal respect. And the latter doctrine, if taken as ethically fundamental, has an implausible air: Nietzschean suspicion that it is a modern ideological artefact looks rather convincing. For in any characteristic that genuinely deserves respect, not least moral goodness or virtue, human beings are clearly unequal. There is then a tendency for the doctrine to shift into a metaphysical or religious dogma. Or it can shift from the actual to the potential: human beings at least all have equal *potential* for virtue, or rationality, etc. That thought is strongly favoured by Mill, and it is one of the reasons why associationist psychology mattered much to him, but it is of course open to empirical refutation.

However, these are not the best ways to think about equal respect. It should not be seen as a matter of religion, metaphysics or psychology, but as expressing the terms of interaction of a state whose citizens have equal civic and political rights. It says that no-one should be treated demeaningly, and no-one should demand deference, just because of who they are, where they come from, or what they do. It requires respect for each person's freedom, in conditions of mutual non-domination. Understood in this way, equality of respect is basic to Mill's liberalism, and the only empirical postulate it requires is that people in general have sufficient rationality and virtue to participate as citizens.

5.4 Mill and liberalism today

On these questions about objectivity and equality there are important differences between Mill's liberalism and leading trends in twentieth-century liberal thought. Liberalism in the twentieth century has made epistemological claims just as liberalism in the nineteenth century did. But they are interestingly reversed. Whereas much nineteenth-century liberalism linked political and civic freedom to an objective ideal of human self-realisation, much twentieth-century liberalism sought to unlink it. Sometimes it sought to base freedom precisely on subjectivism about values. That approach commits the fallacy of thinking one can get a super-value out of denying the objectivity of values. There is a more sophisticated view, however, that says that questions about value will always be contested, as will the very objectivity of such questions, and hence the liberal state should stay out of them, simply guarding the freedom of all who take part in the debate.

Now it follows directly from Mill's Liberty Principle that society has no right to make people do what is for their own good, however right it may be in thinking that it is their good. But it does *not* follow that ethical questions about the good life should be excluded from political discussion of policy. To argue that because an ethical stance is controversial it should not be invoked or debated in the public policy forum is positively peculiar. Debate about controversial questions is precisely what democratic politics is about, and any liberal influenced by Mill will see that as its absolutely indispensable feature. We don't want a political elite deciding what can legitimately appear on the agenda for political discussion. Furthermore, on Mill's principles, a liberal state can legitimately promote conceptions of the good, even though it is barred from enforcing them. We have, Mill says, a duty to educate each other about better ways of living. It breaks no Millian principle to do that through schools and universities, libraries and museums, scientific and artistic activity, advertising campaigns or meetings – all publicly funded by a democratic vote of the citizens. It is not a principle of Millian liberalism that the state should be ethically or aesthetically neutral (though it is another question, of course, whether it is likely to be clumsily counter-productive if it does get involved in some of the above-mentioned ways). Certainly it is no principle of Mill's that the liberal state should not have a conception of the good among its core allegiance-inspiring values.

Twentieth-century liberalism has in general been strongly neutralist; it has not in general been strongly egalitarian. How-ever, there has been an impressive development of strongly ega-litarian liberalism in American philosophy from the 1960s. The Harvard political philosopher, John Rawls, has been the most influential figure. Rawls's political liberalism is also explicitly neutralist; and it must be acknowledged that there is a strongly attractive pragmatic appeal to his search for a broad-church kind of liberalism that can relate to many different ethical ideals – especially in a nation riven by parties and ultimate convictions, and divided into communities. The trouble is that Rawls takes his neutralism to the point where it becomes not a pragmatic policy but a political dogma, and his influence has made people think this dogma virtually definitive of liberalism. To me that seems a step in the wrong direction.

Rawls's theory of justice has been even more influential. It says that the basic structure of a just society should be so organised as to make the worst off as well off as possible. Now liberalism is not defined by its theory of justice, but by the priority it gives to freedom. Yet the theory of justice is important in its own right, and the question of how much continuity there is in this regard between Mill and Rawls is interesting. We have seen that Mill is an economic liberal, in the sense that he strongly endorses the theory of free trade (with some sensible standard qualifications). His arguments for free trade are the classical arguments from economic efficiency. They are separate, as he notes, from his argument for the Liberty Principle; importantly, they are also separate from questions about the ethically optimal distribution of wealth and income. Mill's starting point is philosophically utilitarian, and any specific version of utilitarianism will have a strong drive towards distributive equality of resources built into it, because of plausible empirical propositions about the diminishing marginal utility of income, and the unhappiness caused by relative deprivation. On plausible views of how well-being tracks income either of these is likely to recommend substantially lower levels of resource inequality than actually exist. The only plausible counter, within a Millian framework, would be that large fortunes are important in maintaining standards of excellence against conformity, or the personal independence of individuals against the state. But we have seen (4.3) that Mill's own view is strongly redistributive: he wanted to eliminate fortunes that are large in relation to general wealth, not to preserve them.

So policy in the spirit of Mill would be quite markedly redistributive, while at the same time encouraging competitive markets among private individuals and enterprises. In view of his remarks about the importance of guaranteeing to people the 'essentials of human well-being' (2.5), it would give strong priority to securing minimum levels of resource to all citizens. (Given his characteristic preoccupation with desert, though, he would have wanted to find some way of discriminating against the undeserving poor as well as the undeserving rich.) But Mill's kind of utilitarianism will still differ from Rawls's Difference Principle. It will not rule out the possibility that sufficient gains to overall well-being may sometimes be achieved by a policy that makes the poor somewhat poorer. Thus it does not give the *absolute* priority to the least well-off that Rawls's principle does.

5.5 *What works? What inspires?*

Why read Mill? Liberals can say: he gives the most powerful and comprehensive picture of what liberalism is, strengthens the spirit and provides a moral compass (though, like all moral compasses, a fallible one). Critics of liberalism can say: he gives the most powerful and comprehensive picture of what liberalism is, thereby bringing into focus the strongest version of the enemy.

A simple point in favour of Mill's politics and economics is that it seems to work. Modern democracies have some tendency to approximate to it, at least roughly, and insofar as they do not, it is quite plausible to argue that they would be better off if they did. A Millian social model has as good a chance as any of producing peace, prosperity and free and enjoyable relations of equal respect. The framework of impartial concern for welfare is resilient, even if we give up sum-total utilitarianism. The accent on responsible citizenship is vitally important. The avoidance of mere *modus vivendi* multi-culturalism is wise. Strong protection of liberty of discussion is vital. As for the Liberty Principle, it may often be breached, and in philosophical terms it is rightly controversial, but it still sets down a healthy political guideline that no-one has bettered. Furthermore, when we get to the detail behind these headlines, we find it informed by intelligent and reliable supporting argument.

Still, granting that Millian liberalism works as a political practice, does it inspire as an ethical vision? That is a much more elusive question. It depends on what one thinks of the liberal ideal and the underlying Millian principle (2.3). Can this ideal of self-realisation inspire? Nietzschean perfectionists, communitarians of the left and right, existentialists, religious searchers after transcendence may not be very impressed. It can be accused of being unrealistic about human potential, of putting trust in an objective hierarchy of human values that just isn't there, of glorifying elite individuals or, alternatively, compromising with politics. From the standpoint of more transcendent ideals it looks arrogantly individualist and self-regarding – blind to the deeper reality, which is that the self's final salvation is to be taken up into some greater whole – at the limit, literally *the* Whole. In a more down-to-earth version of that thought, and perhaps more soberingly for liberals, one can argue that, for all its noble vision, the liberal ideal inevitably coarsens into self-assertion and a meaningless emphasis on being 'different'.

There is a case for the defence, however. Mill's focus on *human* goods – happiness, spontaneity, independence – is civilised and attainable in the world as it is. It does not sacralise suffering or treat enjoyment with suspicion. It is not posited on some wishful thinking that is impossible to discuss. Unlike unattainably overblown self-images, or still worse, the violent and totalitarian utopian visions that people so depressingly sell out to, it flows not from moral weakness but from moral strength. Or so it seems to me. But I must leave it to the reader to decide.

FURTHER READING

Writings by Mill

There is now a very fine edition of Mill's collected works: *Collected Works of John Stuart Mill*, general editor, John M. Robson. 33 vols, London: Routledge, 1963–91. The introductions to individual volumes are authoritative and helpful. Volume 33 comprises a variety of indexes to the collected works as a whole.

The most readily available of Mill's ethical and political works are *Utilitarianism, Liberty, Considerations on Representative Government, The Subjection of Women,* and (the unfinished, posthumous) *Chapters on Socialism*. These exist in various editions. The *Autobiography*, together with the twin essays on 'Bentham' and 'Coleridge', provides an excellent introduction to Mill's general outlook on liberalism, conservatism and modernity.

Also interesting are his study of 'Auguste Comte and Positivism', and his two critical essays on 'De Tocqueville on Democracy in America'. The *Principles of Political Economy* contain much of his social philosophy as well as his economics.

Mill's reputation as moral and political philosopher has never stood higher; but his overall standing as a philosopher is still underestimated, for a variety of interesting reasons (I discuss some of them in my Introduction to *The Cambridge Companion to John Stuart Mill*). This is changing, as historians of philosophy become more aware of the many continuities between his views and current debates in the philosophy of language, logic, mathematics and science. Mill's treatments of these subjects are in *A System of*

Logic and in the unmemorably titled *An Examination of Sir William Hamilton's Philosophy*. The latter also contains his influential phenomenalist analysis of matter as 'the permanent possibility of sensation'. Mill's philosophical views on religion can be studied in his *Three Essays on Religion*.

Writings about Mill in general

Alan Ryan, *J.S. Mill*, London: Routledge, 1975.

John Skorupski, *John Stuart Mill*, London: Routledge, 1989.

——(ed.) *The Cambridge Companion to John Stuart Mill*, Cambridge: Cambridge University Press, 1998.

Stafford, William, *John Stuart Mill*, London: Macmillan, 1998.

Ryan (1975), Skorupski (1998) and Stafford (1998) cover all aspects of his thought, while Skorupski (1989) focuses on his philosophy.

Biographies of J.S. Mill

Nicholas Capaldi, *John Stuart Mill*, Cambridge: Cambridge University Press, 2004.

Michael St. John Packe, *The Life of John Stuart Mill*, London: Secker & Warburg, 1954.

On Mill's moral and political philosophy

Fred R. Berger, *Happiness, Justice and Freedom: The Moral and Political Philosophy of John Stuart Mill*, London: University of California Press, 1984.

Wendy Donner, *The Liberal Self: John Stuart Mill's Moral and Political Philosophy*, Ithaca, NY: Cornell University Press, 1991.

Further reading for Chapter 2

Roger Crisp, *Mill on Utilitarianism*, London: Routledge, 1997.

David Lyons, *Rights, Welfare, and Mill's Moral Theory*, Oxford: Oxford University Press, 1994.

Henry West, *An Introduction to Mill's Utilitarian Ethics*, Cambridge: Cambridge University Press, 2004.

——(ed.), *The Blackwell Guide to Mill's Utilitarianism*, Oxford: Blackwell, 2005.

West (2005) contains essays on, together with the text of, Mill's *Utilitarianism*.

Further reading for Chapter 3

John Gray and G. W. Smith (eds.), *John Stuart Mill's On Liberty in Focus*, London: Routledge, 1991.

Alan S. Kahan, *Aristocratic Liberalism: The Social and Political Thought of Jacob Burckhardt, John Stuart Mill, and Alexis de Tocqueville*, Oxford: Oxford University Press, 1992.

Jonathan Riley, *Mill on Liberty*, London: Routledge, 1998.

Gray and Smith contains essays on, together with the text of, Mill's *On Liberty*.

Further reading for Chapter 4

J. H. Burns, 'J. S. Mill and democracy, 1829–61', in J. B. Schneewind (ed.) *Mill: A Collection of Critical Essays*, London: Macmillan, 1968.

Graeme Duncan, *Marx and Mill: Two Views of Social Conflict and Social Harmony*, Cambridge: Cambridge University Press, 1973.

Dennis F. Thompson, *John Stuart Mill and Representative Government*, Princeton, NJ: Princeton University Press, 1976.

INDEX